In Hot

In Hot

*Memoir of a Marine
Huey Pilot in Vietnam*

Joseph L. Hutton, Jr.

McFarland & Company, Inc., Publishers
Jefferson, North Carolina

ISBN (print) 978-1-4766-9742-0
ISBN (ebook) 978-1-4766-5511-6

Library of Congress cataloging data are available

© 2025 Joseph L. Hutton, Jr. All rights reserved

No part of this book may be reproduced or transmitted in any form or by any means, electronic or mechanical, including photocopying or recording, or by any information storage and retrieval system, without permission in writing from the publisher.

Front cover image: a colorized version of a U.S. Marine Corps Bell UH-1E *Huey* takes off from guided missile cruiser USS *Topeka* (CLG-8) off Vietnam, in 1966 (U.S. Navy photo).

Printed in the United States of America

*McFarland & Company, Inc., Publishers
Box 611, Jefferson, North Carolina 28640
www.mcfarlandpub.com*

For my wife, Paula.
She has been a rock
putting up with my nonsense!

And for my sons, Josh and Chris,
because I wanted them to know.

Table of Contents

Acknowledgments	x
Preface	1
Prologue: Republic of Vietnam, Midsummer 1970	5
1. Moberly Junior College: Moberly, Missouri, 1966	7
2. Boot Camp, Marine Corps Recruit Depot: San Diego, California, 1966	12
3. Naval Air Station, Memphis: Millington, Tennessee, Fall 1966	18
4. Keesler Air Force Base: Biloxi, Mississippi, 1966–1967	20
5. Marine Corps Air Station: Beaufort, South Carolina, 1967	23
6. OCS, Marine Corps Base: Quantico, Virginia, 1968	28
7. The Basic School, MCB: Quantico, Virginia, Summer 1968	33
8. U.S. Army Primary Flight Training: Ft. Wolters, Texas, Fall 1968	38
9. Advanced Flight Training, Hunter Army Airfield and Ft. Stewart: Savannah, Georgia, Early 1969	43
10. Final Qualification, MCAS(H) Santa Ana: Tustin, California, 1969	48
11. Moberly, Missouri: Fall 1969	52
12. En Route to Vietnam: Fall 1969	54
13. South Vietnam: October 21, 1969–September 30, 1970	56
14. First Flight	64
15. Qualifications and Designations	74

Table of Contents

16. Experiments with Weapons	76
17. Intramural and Social Activities	79
18. Bob Hope Entertains the Troops	84
19. Rest and Relaxation: Sydney, Australia, January 1970	93
20. Control Problems	95
21. Lost Camera	99
22. Dings on the Tail Rotor	103
23. Night Fright or Which Way Is Up?	106
24. Eagle Claw or What Country Is This?	110
25. April Fools	117
26. Sniffing Out the Enemy	119
27. Rockets Across the Demilitarized Zone	123
28. Magnet Ass	125
29. Reviewing the Troops	127
30. Hogs and Napalm	130
31. Crew Rest	132
32. Meritorious Copilot	135
33. Troop Insert	139
34. A Flight Demonstration	142
35. Rocket Practice	145
36. Night Medevac: June 10 and 11, 1970	148
37. Section Lead	155
38. Cold Cokes Served on a Mountaintop	156
39. Recon Rescue	159
40. Recon and Tigers—Oh My!	163
41. How to Become the O Club Officer in Two Easy Steps	166
42. Guns, Guns, More Guns and Some Slick Hops	169
43. The Squadron Duty Officer	171
44. Twenty-Four Coke Grenades	175
45. Oil Can Bombs	177
46. III Marine Amphibious Force	179

47. Fishing the Explosive Way	181
48. Orange Basketballs	183
49. The Miss America USO Show	185
50. Overloaded Medevac	188
51. Returning the Navy	191
52. How High Can You Go?	194
53. Another Painful Loss	196
54. Winning the Hearts and Minds	199
55. Farewell Dinner	202
56. Home at Last: October 1970	205
57. Semper Fidelis	208
Appendix A: Numbered Call Signs, After April 9, 1970	211
Appendix B: III MAF Command Chronology Civic Action, August 1970	212
Appendix C: III MAF Command Chronology Civic Action, September 1970	216
Appendix D: Monthly Flight Time	220
Bibliography	221
Index	223

Acknowledgments

This book covers events of October 1969 to September 1970 as best as I can remember them. It is not fiction; these are real stories. Every Marine in HML-167 was my friend, and nothing in here is intended to bring disrespect to them or to insult them. Remember, I am old, and my memory isn't what it once was. Many friends have jogged memories, and I have included their thoughts.

I would like to thank several people for starting me on this project:

My son Chris, for encouraging me to get started and sharing our OCD.

My eldest cousin Leo Hutton for the first proofreading and offering several suggestions.

The Naval Institute Press for reading my first efforts and sending me to McFarland. To McFarland for encouraging me to fill out missing chapters.

Major Brian Griffing, USMC (Ret), Senior Marine JROTC Instructor, Lejeune High School, for encouraging me.

Major Tom Broderick, USMC, for supplying numerous after-action reports from our year together and for supplying a few addresses of long-lost friends, who then provided more addresses and contacts. Without those contacts, this would be a very short story.

Col MA1 Smith, Capt Injun Joe Hall, Capt Uncle Milty Matthews, Capt John Gale, LtCol Larry Grandy, Capt Lynn Boyer, LtCol Fudd Davis, LtCol Jenks Jenkins and LtCol Paul Pratt for sharing your stories and critical insight, most important, supplementing my meager recall.

LtCol Harold Walker USMCR (Ret) and author of *The Grotto*, Books One and Two for allowing the use of his resources and giving me a good first read. Hal was a member of HMM-262, Chatterbox 28, during this time frame and a member of HML-776 when I was assigned as an advisor to the reserve Marines in Chicago.

Col Slick Katz, who sent me to the Texas Tech Archives and caused a complete rewrite of this effort.

Preface

Through twenty-five years in the Marine Corps, more than twenty-three and a half of which was as a naval aviator, I've managed to live through some scary moments—being shot at (multiple times), engine failures (multiple times), inadvertent flight into crappy weather (multiple times) and long overwater flights with neither navigation aid nor radio contact (multiple times). None of them were more frequent or scarier than in my year in combat.

Many times, I have been asked what Vietnam was like. My usual wiseass comment was "It was hours and hours of boredom punctuated by moments of stark terror." Many of our missions never drew fire or had enemy contact. We circled for hours watching over the Phrogs as they delivered food, water and ammunition to troops in the field. On many days and nights, we waited on standby missions for whatever was to come. When it got interesting, it got really interesting: heart rates were up and sweat was running down our backs.

In our off-hours, we played intramural football, sat around the ready room playing Acey-Deucy, or frequented the officers' club. Some days, we actually worked, performing our additional duties.

The weather was either hot and wet or hot and dry. I was issued "wet-weather gear," which I still have. I don't remember many wet days, but I know we had them. There was a monsoon season that should have impacted our activities, but we flew anyway. Command chronologies from that time frame refer to flight ops being restricted; I just don't recall not flying because of weather. The reason we were there was to support the troops in the field. We flew at night without night-vision goggles; we flew in the day, whatever the weather.

Our resources for communication and navigation in the aircraft were limited compared with what is available today. We had a single ultrahigh-frequency (UHF) radio for communicating with other aircraft, with air traffic control (ATC) and with mission controllers. We had a single FM radio for communication with the ground forces. Navigation aids included a tactical air navigation (TACAN) and an automatic direction finder (ADF). The TACAN provided a bearing and distance to a fixed station, usually located at or near an airfield. The ADF also provided a bearing but not distance to the broadcast station and was special to us because of its frequency range. It received signals that extended into the same AM range as Armed Forces Radio, so we were able to listen to rock and roll while we worked. I still listen to '60s and '70s rock today!

Most missions we launched with a full crew of two pilots, a crew chief and a gunner. VIP missions we had either one or two pilots and a crew chief. We always had a crew chief and he was the one resource that I used every day.

There were many standard missions that we performed each day. We always provided a slick (unarmed UH-1E outfitted with a VIP kit) for the commanding generals of III Marine Amphibious Force (III MAF), First Marine Division (1st MarDiv), First Marine Air Wing (1st MAW) and chief of staff of III MAF. The Korean regiment south of Marble Mountain got an unarmed Huey without the VIP kit. The regimental headquarters of the Fifth and Seventh Marines also got a slick UH-1E and a Phrog (CH-46) for whatever the regiment needed on a daily basis.

There was always a section of guns (two armed UH-1Es) on standby for medevac support in 12-hour shifts and another section on quick-reaction standby, known as Mission 80. As nonstandard missions we were also frequently assigned regimental resupply escort missions, recon support and various VIP support flights. From December 1969 through the middle of June 1970, we provided a section of guns in support of MACV—SOG, its assigned mission number, Mission 72 and known as Eagle Claw. In the last couple of months of our support for Eagle Claw, we only provided a slick Huey as mission commander; the guns were provided by HML-367 with the very capable Cobras. We provided air transportation for the Bob Hope and Miss America USO shows and occasionally transported various commanders to either the USNS *Sanctuary* or USNS *Repose* hospital ships to check on their troops.

The standard missions could be written into the flight schedule early, but all the additional missions came in after 10:00 p.m., so it was usually 1:00 a.m. before the schedule was finished and distributed each day. This was well before the advent of computers, so the flight schedule was prepared on a manual typewriter and duplicated on a hand-cranked mimeograph machine.

Although I didn't fly every day, I did fly most days. There were many days I flew 12 or more hours; most months I flew 70 or more hours, some months, much more. By the end of my tour, I had accumulated nearly 1,000 hours of combat flight time with over 300 hours of that at night, well before the advent of night-vision goggles. At the end of that year, I had been awarded 41 strike/flight Air Medals representing over 800 combat missions and one single mission Air Medal.

Our company grade officers took pride in being where we needed to be to provide support. We thought our field grade officers were too cautious and we bristled anytime restrictions were placed on us. Probably, we let our inexperience lead us into situations that were over our heads. We worked them out. We learned fast. When the crap hit the fan, we responded. We were bulletproof until we weren't. We became friends and we lost friends.

Most of these "moments of stark terror" came when I was actively flying on a daily basis, both as a company grade officer and in the first few years as a field grade officer. I have attempted to recall for you those times that got my heart beating faster than normal. My path from college to Marine aviation, I think, was unusual. I have included it here as an example of a saying I try to live by: "When you reach the bottom of the hole, stop digging."

I mention a few people in here that I have great respect for. Some I included because of the senior billet they held; anyone could do the research to find their identities. I have included the names of friends when I could get their permission or their nicknames when I couldn't get ahold of them. They were all included to show my respect for their contributions to the safety of this great nation and, in some cases, to share their stories of terror, especially when it augments a story I was trying to relate. I may have left a few out that I could not remember; you know who you are. I respect and admire you! I also recognize Marines who made the ultimate sacrifice; tributes to them are at the end of the chapter where their exploits are recounted.

On every flight we reported to Direct Air Support Center (DASC) when we were outbound on a mission, when we had trouble on a mission and when we were inbound, mission complete. We also had to contact Helicopter Direction Center (HDC) for clearances through areas where indirect fire (artillery and mortars) was being utilized.

At times throughout history, the Marine Corps has renamed existing units and subunits, mostly because their mission changed or to incorporate current verbiage. Units were restructured to facilitate better use of assets. Flying Groups (MAG) had a Headquarters and Maintenance Squadron (H&MS) and a Marine Air Base Squadron (MABS). H&MS became Marine Aircraft and Logistics Squadron (MALS) and MABS was moved to the Marine Wing Support Group (MWSG) becoming the Marine Wing Support Squadron (MWSS). MAF and MEF are one example of renaming to support a mission change. From 1965 until 1988, the Marine Corps had "amphibious" forces; thus, we had MAF, MAB and MAU or Marine Amphibious Force, Marine Amphibious Brigade and Marine Amphibious Unit. These were all "combined arms" units—that is, these were aviation and ground forces combined to accomplish a specific mission. In 1988, amphibious forces became expeditionary forces. So now we have MEF, MEB and MEU or Marine Expeditionary Force, Marine Expeditionary Brigade and Marine Expeditionary Unit. MAF/MEF was comprised of a combination of division/wing size units, MAB/MEB was regiment/group and MAU/MEU was battalion/squadron.

"In hot" refers to the radio call a gunship makes when the pilot rolls his aircraft into an attack and arms his weapons, be they guns or rockets. The next call the pilot would make is "Off left" or "Off right," which indicates the direction he is pulling off the target and that his weapons are safe. In a sustained attack, the next call would be "Two's in hot," meaning his wingman is now in the attack. That sequence would be repeated until the target is destroyed or the aircraft are "winchester" which indicates the aircraft are out of ammunition.

Prologue
Republic of Vietnam, Midsummer 1970

Bright orange and red tracers rose slowly through the darkness, expanding to the size of softballs, then seemed to streak by outside our helicopter's windows as the village below us suffered repeated explosions in the four quadrants formed by the east-west river and the north-south highway. The tracers that you could see added excitement, but the worries came from the four rounds between them that you couldn't see. I was at the controls of our UH-1E "Huey" gunship maneuvering to position for a firing run, communicating with the ground unit on FM, listening to '60s rock and protest songs on the ADF while the pilot worked the UHF radio, coordinating the arrival of the two Medevac CH-46 "Phrogs" out of Marble Mountain, our home base here in I Corps in South Vietnam, setting up firing runs from "Spooky," the U.S. Air Force AC-117 gun bird, deconflicting traffic, getting flair drops from "Basketball," the Marine KC-130 from VMGR-152 flair ship supporting us, all while monitoring the position of our wingman, ensuring that he was in position and assisting with what needed doing—that is, suppressing fire so the 46s could get into the zone. It was going to be a long night. The Marines on the ground were reporting multiple emergency medevacs, and there seemed to be no end to the assault taking place.

The captain paused to yell over the intercom, "Hutton, if you hadn't screwed up your last mission, you could be flying wing instead of copilot. Then I could count on you being where I need you and doing what I need done. Instead, I'm jumping through my ass wondering what our wing is doing and hoping he does what I need."

The captain was right of course, but I was too busy to answer. I was focused on putting some rockets into a mortar firing position while avoiding return fire. I had the Huey in a dive, power on, ball centered and sights aligned, as I squeezed off a pair of 2.75-inch folding fin aerial rockets with 17-pound warheads at the troubling mortar position. I pulled off to the left to avoid overflying the position and directing our door gunners to fire their M-60s to cover our pull. I noted the rocket strikes, pleased to see that there were several secondary explosions. That should take care of that problem. Looking for my next target, I needed to get some 7.62 mm rounds into the multiple targets around the village from the four forward-firing M-60 machine guns mounted on our gunship. We needed to suppress much more enemy fire before the Phrogs start hauling medevacs out of this hellhole.

1

Moberly Junior College
Moberly, Missouri, 1966

In Moberly, our school structure was unique. The town had six elementary schools scattered around town serving grades K–7. During my sixth-grade year, they reopened a facility that years before had been the "black" school and consolidated the seventh grade from all six of the elementary schools into that one building. My class was the first to participate. Another building had eighth, ninth and tenth grades, and still another combined the last two years of high school with the two years of a junior college. Many of my high school habits carried over into that junior college.

My first summer after high school, my dad's brother helped me get a job with the Missouri Department of Highways. Every summer they hired several young men to work various positions on road crews. These positions were hourly and paid very well since we were working from about six in the morning until sundown. My uncle thought I might want to make the highway department a career, so he got me a salaried position. If I had approached it as a career opportunity, that would have been great except I wasn't ready to settle down, so I sort of took it in the shorts pay-wise that summer and the next.

We were putting a coat of asphalt on top of the old concrete that constituted US 63 North from Moberly to the Macon County line, a distance of about 16 miles. My task was to ensure the finished pavement was level and smooth. To do that, I operated a 15-foot aluminum bar that looked like a miniature I beam. It had an aluminum wheel on each end, a long handle to push it with and three adjustable, pointed bolts spaced through the bottom of the beam.

Each morning, I ran a string from wheel to wheel and set the bolts so that they were an eighth of an inch from the string. Then when the "finish" roller was done, I would push the beam along the roadway. If the bolts dragged anywhere, the asphalt had to be rolled repeatedly until it passed this test.

Other crewmen tested the thickness and compactness of the asphalt, the temperature of the asphalt as it came off the truck and still another measured the size of the rock that went into the mix. Like many government jobs there was a lot of standing around waiting to perform your specific task. My waiting position was sitting on the last roller with its operator and watching traffic go by.

As many people know, US 63 is a north-south highway that runs from Minnesota through the Lake of the Ozarks in southern Missouri. Many young people traveled that route to their vacation spot on the lake; some were even getting a head start on their tanning. We saw a few young ladies in convertibles with more than just the car top down working on that tan without lines, and they were surprised by the construction delays. So even though the pay wasn't great, the visual benefits were excellent.

The fall of 1964, after high school, I enrolled at Moberly Junior College (now it would be called a community college, and it has been renamed to Moberly Area Community College). My classes were mostly basic foundation classes with the addition of French, accounting and some advanced math. Except for freshman English, I did OK on my grades; nothing spectacular, but I was getting by. As spring approached, several friends and I made excursions to the old strip mine area northwest of Moberly. There were some great areas there for boating, swimming and some decent beaches to lie on, if you brought a friend. Liquor and beer were easy to obtain; nobody was checking IDs then.

In my junior year of high school, I tried out for and was accepted into the "MOJUCO Singers," a 30-voice a cappella group whose members came from all four years of the school. We performed for various groups locally and each year took a weeklong bus trip out of state performing along the way. As evidence of my lack of industry, my sophomore year at Moberly Junior College I dropped out of the group for absolutely no good reason other than my lack of direction.

The summer between my freshman and sophomore years I was back working with the highway department, this time in an area west of Macon where they were pouring new concrete. My job was report writing, based on information that was furnished to me. I didn't like it much and after a few weeks I quit.

For the rest of the summer, I assisted teaching Red Cross swimming lessons. I was an accomplished swimmer, having achieved several merit badges in swimming while I was in Boy Scouts. This was much better for me.

1. Moberly Junior College

I continued at Moberly Junior College the next fall (1965), taking classes in biology, zoology and calculus. My grades slipped some more as I didn't do well in zoology, calculus or my final freshman English requirements.

I was a sophomore at Moberly Junior College, living at home, driving a delivery car for Southside Cleaners, making about $20 a week plus the pint of vodka the owner left for me every Saturday night on the back step of the cleaners, living the dream—that is, never missing a party, avoiding homework. I had just finished my third semester of freshman English and was into the fourth semester of college. That third semester of freshman English requires some explanation. Two semesters are required to complete the academic curriculum. My first semester English professor was of foreign descent and spoke numerous languages. Her favorite author was Thomas Wolfe; he wasn't my favorite, and the semester final only had two questions, both about Wolfe. Since one was an opinion question, I provided mine, which didn't exactly jive with her opinion. Needless to say, I got to repeat that class next semester.

In January of my fourth semester, I got home from school late, a normal occurrence for me. Mom was in the kitchen. She announced, "You've got mail."

I looked on the kitchen table; there it was, a fat, legal-sized envelope from the US government. I didn't think much about it; not a lot bothered me. I was driving a '53 Chevy that Mom's brother, my uncle Floyd, helped me keep running. Again, not a lot bothered me until I opened the envelope; the letter started out in bold lettering, "**Congratulations: You've been reclassified from 2S to 1A.**"

The letter went on to explain that 2S was a student deferment from the military draft and that to keep the deferment, I had to maintain a 2.0 grade point average in school and my 1.9 wasn't cutting it.

In 1966, we were a few years into the Vietnam War, and it would continue for several more. The draft was active and a 1A classification meant that you were at the top of the list for selection. The government included a second letter in the same envelope instructing me to report for a physical in 30 days. My goose was cooked. There was no way to get my rather anemic 1.9 GPA up to a 2.0; new grades wouldn't come out until May, and this was only late January.

This all started years before. I didn't do the work I did not get great grades in high school. I played football, ran track, chased girls and just got by, not because I wasn't capable; I just didn't do the work. I performed exceptionally well on all "standardized" tests such as the "California Achievement Test," but I didn't get good grades. I just didn't do the work.

Every night on the news they were announcing the number of soldier deaths in Vietnam. I knew I didn't want to be in the army. My first stop was at the Navy/Marine Corps recruiting station. The navy recruiter, whom I wanted to talk to, was at lunch, but the Marine was there. I'm the kind of guy that if I was standing by a lake, you could sell me a bucket of water, and that Marine could sell water! I never made it to the air force recruiter, nor did I see the navy guy. The Marine explained that I could enlist on a 120-day delay plan. If I did that, I could sign on and not have to report to boot camp for 120 days; that would allow me to finish my fourth semester of college, which he said would open opportunities later. He also explained that the Marines always brought their casualties home (he didn't differentiate between wounded and killed). I was in no hurry to go, and that sounded like a good deal, so I signed up.

My recruiter also explained that since I had some college, I should sign up for an aviation contract. I resisted him on the aviation contract. After all, if you are going to be a Marine, you're going to be an "in-the-mud fighting man." I eventually relented. The aviation package guaranteed that my military occupational specialty (MOS) or job would be somewhere in the aviation field, depending on my abilities. As it turned out, both the 120-day delay and the aviation contract really paid off.

My physical was set for a couple of weeks later in St. Louis, where I would also take some qualifying tests. My report date for boot camp was July 1, 1966. Now all I had to do was finish my fourth semester and tell Mom and Dad that I had joined the Marines. Dad was a flight engineer in B-24s in World War II. He flew out of England, deep into Germany, so the aviation contract sounded pretty good to him. Mom wasn't so sure; however, she knew I wasn't accomplishing much where I was.

My sophomore yearbook picture from Moberly Junior College.

1. Moberly Junior College

I was sworn into the Marine Corps Reserve on March 3, 1966. During the processing, I filled out a medical history that stated I'd had asthma since I was six months old. The recruiter told me that if I really wanted to be a Marine, I needed to leave that information off the form and gave me a new form to fill out. I never realized that my asthma was "disqualifying" for all branches of service. I could have been exempted from the draft and stayed home. I'm glad I didn't know about that option.

Over the next four months I got my physical, finished my fourth semester of junior college, attended the NJCAA basketball tournament in Hutchinson, Kansas, where my school won the first of two consecutive national championships (the team was coached by Cotton Fitzsimmons, who later coached the Atlanta Hawks and the Phoenix Suns; he was also my junior college PE teacher).

While in Hutchinson I attempted to buy some liquor and was "carded" for the first time. Missouri's driver's license was paper with the date in blue ink. I realized that if I was careful, I could scrape the left side of the six in 1946 (my birth year) and with a blue pencil I could complete the conversion to 1943. Suddenly I was three years older, and that was plenty good for Kansas.

As soon as school was out for the summer, I traveled to Ardmore, Oklahoma, for the American Red Cross water safety instructors course, then taught swimming lessons through June. Oh, I also got my GPA up to a magnificent 1.95.

2

Boot Camp, Marine Corps Recruit Depot

San Diego, California, 1966

Mom and Dad took me to St. Louis the evening of June 30, 1966. I reported to the processing center the next morning for some final paperwork and swearing into the active-duty United States Marine Corps. I saw Mom and Dad for the last time until boot camp graduation just before we boarded a TWA airplane for the flight west.

I was going to boot camp in San Diego. Wow. I would be a Hollywood Marine, issued sunglasses and a surfboard (or so goes the story told by Parris Island Marines). I was looking forward to this (I didn't really believe the sunglasses and surfboard bit, but how bad could it be?). I had been in Boy Scouts, was a "Life Scout," had the God and Country Award, was in Order of the Arrow and had participated in some pretty rugged camping. My Scoutmaster was a former army infantry officer and he helped prepare me for boot camp. I spent time in the woods, hunted, played football and ran track in high school, attended the Red Cross water safety instructors course and taught swimming lessons for the last month of my freedom. I was in pretty good physical condition.

That thought was shattered as we hit the yellow footprints and were greeted by a non-smiling, red-faced, screaming Marine gunnery sergeant. Life as I had known it was over! Our welcome to Platoon 2055 consisted of a 30-second haircut that was little more than a scalping and an initial issue of utilities, boots, socks, underwear and a duffel bag. Combat training gear, including an M-14 rifle, two canteens, a bayonet and scabbard, a first aid kit and web gear including belt, two cloth canteen covers, a canteen cup, two canteens, and first aid kit was next, then off to our quarters lugging our sea bags with 50 or more pounds of gear. Our quarters for the next eight weeks were a series of open bay Quonset

2. Boot Camp, Marine Corps Recruit Depot

huts with multiple rows of two-high bunk beds (called racks by Marines everywhere). At the foot of each row of racks were footlockers, where we stored everything we weren't wearing.

We packed the clothing we had worn on the flight to San Diego in boxes provided, wrote a short note to our parents, sealed the boxes and said goodbye to civilian life. We weren't Marines yet; we'd been sworn in, but that was only a formality. We were "maggots" as we were told many times over the next eight weeks. The kindest thing we were called was "recruit." Most of us would become Marines, but it would be an exhausting process.

Our initial training crew consisted of a gunnery sergeant (GySgt), staff sergeant (SSgt) and a sergeant (Sgt). During our twelve weeks of training, the SSgt and Sgt were each promoted one rank.

On our first full day, we were taken to the post exchange (PX) were we bought shower shoes, shaving gear, soap, towels and wash cloths, brass polish, starch, cleaning equipment for our rifles and a tablet of paper to take notes during training and for writing to our loved ones. Our first trip to the head (in the Navy and Marine Corps, a bathroom facility is called a head; the Army calls it a latrine; and in the Air Force, it is the ladies' room) we wore our boots in the shower to soften them and shape them to our feet. We were taught to shower and shave in 15 minutes or less while cleaning the area behind us.

Our first effort at marching was a ragged attempt, after instruction on which foot we stepped off on (left) and the length of stride (30 inches); it was marked by several halts, punctuated by push-ups, sit ups and squat thrusts and a lot of focused yelling. We finally figured which was our left foot and what a constant 30-inch step felt like. Close order drill, classes in Marine history, more close order drill, physical fitness training, more close order drill, first aid training, swim training, water survival training, more close order drill, more fitness training, runs of three miles or more in formation and cleaning our equipment made up our day (every day).

As one of the recruits in our platoon with some college, I was appointed scribe and remedial instructor. My job was to take any notes the drill instructors (DIs) needed and assist other recruits with retention of information we were provided in our academic classes.

We were taught how to address our DIs: "Sir, the private requests permission to speak to the drill instructor, sir," or if we need to go to the duty hut after knocking three times (big thundering fists on the hatch), it was, "Sir, the private requests permission to enter the duty hut, sir." On the second or third day as scribe, I needed to ask a question of my DI who was in the duty hut. After pounding on the hatch, I managed to screw up the speech and was told to assume the front leaning rest position and to begin push-ups. After about 15 or 20 minutes, the DI came out, realized he had forgotten about me as I was counting through push-up number 100 (my physical conditioning from Ardmore really paid off). Our first time on the pull-up bars, I performed about 17 quality pull-ups. This pleased our DI since it was obvious I was not going to be a fitness problem.

In the first couple of weeks, we were marched to the medical facility where we lined up for shots. Both arms were subjected to multiple vaccinations, such as smallpox, yellow fever, polio, measles, mumps, typhoid and tetanus. During my physical exam, it was determined that I needed glasses (I had worn them while in college) and I was issued two pairs of glasses. We called them "birth control glasses" because there was no way to get a date while wearing the super ugly, black framed glasses the military issued at the time.

At one point in an early formation, the DI called out anyone who had some college. Since I was one of those, he wanted to know if any of us were interested in becoming an officer. Unfortunately, I was still 19 and not yet eligible. To qualify, one had to be 20 when they applied and 21 by the time they were commissioned. I was told to "Get back in line!"

We didn't know it, but every halt while marching was planned down to the last minute to include fitness training. We woke each morning well before sunup to the screams of our DI, went through our morning routine of shaving, showering, sh*tting, then marched to the chow hall. We ate fast and learned to sleep standing at parade rest outside the chow hall while the last of our platoon finished eating and we were rejoined by our DIs. Many times after eating, I recall standing outside the mess hall (the air force and army called them dining facilities) at parade rest with my eyes closed, catching an additional couple of minutes of shut-eye. We ate well, and skinny guys like me were encouraged to ingest plenty of calories and hopefully put on some weight.

Each platoon was divided into four squads with one person from each squad selected to be the squad leader. A fifth person from the platoon was selected as platoon guide (a marching position at the head of the platoon). The guide also carried the guidon anytime we were performing close order drill. I was selected as one of the first squad leaders and held that position until the middle of our fifth week of training. Squad leaders were routinely fired for screw-ups within their squad or for their own incompetence. My turn was coming, not for any of the above reasons, but because it was time. Everything the DIs did was scripted, and at some point, everything would change.

During the fourth week of training, we moved by bus to Edson

2. Boot Camp, Marine Corps Recruit Depot

Range at Camp Pendleton for rifle qualification. The first week there, each platoon was assigned either mess duty or butts duty. In "butts" duty, we would work in the receiving end of the rifle range, servicing and scoring the targets as the platoon that was firing worked to get better with their rifles. Our platoon got butts duty (much better than mess duty, which involved washing serving trays and cleaning the mess hall). As one of the squad leaders working in the butts, I had no assigned duties except for supervising the efforts of the recruits in my squad. While walking up and down the butts (which was the impact end of the rifle range), I was offered some coffee by one of the Marines on full-time duty at the rifle range. It was my first time for "Irish" infused coffee; it really hit the spot, also highly inappropriate. If reported, the corporal could have been relieved of duty and been given office hours (nonjudicial punishment administered by his commanding officer) or possibly a court-martial. There are three levels of court-martial (a legal proceeding similar to civilian trial): a summary court-martial (a single officer serving as judge and jury), a special court-martial (a three-officer panel) and a general court-martial (a five-officer panel). These differ by the level of punishment each can apply and the number of officers (and sometimes enlisted men) assigned to the court.

Life at Edson Range was different than at MCRD. We still marched everywhere we went, but we had graduated to an open squad bay-type barracks instead of the Quonset huts we had been in. Our platoon was assigned to the second deck of one of the several barracks.

Our fifth week was snapping in, dry-firing our rifles to get used to the shooting positions and squeezing the trigger without the recoil. Painful hours in the shooting positions, primarily the prone, kneeling and squatting positions. It was an endless, boring week! This was the week our DI destroyed the barracks, turned over the racks (Marines sleep in racks, not beds), dumped our footlockers and generally shattered our world. The guide and all the squad leaders were "fired" and replaced with other recruits (in addition to being "maggots" we were "recruits" until we could earn the title Marine). I learned later this was a planned event, meant to "shake up" the platoon.

Week six was live fire, four days of firing followed by qualification day. Marines have four levels of qualification, ranging from unqualified to marksman (the lowest level of acceptable qualification), then sharpshooter and finally expert (the best qualification a Marine can get unless he becomes a team shooter). I qualified "sharpshooter," same as the "Texas tower" shooter of August 1966. My requalification later was "expert," and I qualified "expert" every year for the next 24 years. I still remember the commands given on the range: "All ready on the right. All ready on the left. All ready on the firing line. You may load. Commence firing!"

After we finished the rifle range, our lead DI was fired for coming to work drunk and we were assigned another GySgt to supervise our training. We had a difficult time adjusting to his rhythm during close order drill, and at some point, our platoon leader recognized this and removed the new gunny and assigned our original SSgt, now GySgt, to lead the rest of our training.

The last two weeks featured more marching, more running, more physical training, more classes and more shaping of our minds and bodies. We had the opportunity to attend church services on Sunday mornings. Having been a constant churchgoer, I took advantage of the opportunity and attended Protestant services every chance I got. Our physical training included swim/water survival training. With my experiences in the water, both with Boy Scouts and the Red Cross, this was easy for me.

We were also fitted for "Charlie" and "Alpha" uniforms during the last weeks of boot camp. A "Charlie" uniform was a short-sleeve dress shirt and dress slacks, both Marine tan. The "Alpha" uniform was a long-sleeve dress shirt, dress slacks and a blouse (in the Marines, a suit coat is called a blouse), also tan and identical blouse and slacks in forest green.

During this time, I worked my way back to being a squad leader. As we approached graduation, we had a drill competition where our platoon finished first among the several platoons graduating together. The performance of the guide and squad leaders was instrumental in obtaining this recognition.

After a brief interview by a panel of officers, it was announced that I and the other three squad

My boot camp graduation photograph.

2. Boot Camp, Marine Corps Recruit Depot

leaders and the guide would be awarded the rank of private first class, meritoriously, and the guide would be given a dress blue uniform. Our actual promotion date was September 1, 1966, with boot camp graduation on September 3. I had entered boot camp as a rather scrawny 132-pound youngster and graduated as a 150-pound lean, mean Marine. I was now making a hearty $96.20 per month plus a $4 monthly clothing allowance.

My mom and dad flew out to San Diego for our graduation. Mom had several cousins living in the Los Angeles/Santa Monica area. So after graduation, they visited with them before returning to Missouri. Our visit was brief, but I was really happy to have them there.

Infantry training regiment (ITR) followed boot camp and was at Camp Pendleton, located between San Diego and Los Angeles. "Every Marine a rifleman" is one of several sayings that apply to all Marines. So all Marines get training as a basic infantry man before getting a final MOS.

ITR was formal training in squad tactics, exposure to the gas chamber and other basic Marine skills. For those on aviation contracts, it was only half as long as for the non-aviation Marines, but the Marine Corps can pack a lot into those few weeks.

Movements from the barracks to various ranges for specialty training was either marching in formation for close ranges or by "cattle car" (a semi-tractor trailer combination, where the trailer is an open boxcar with wooden bench seating and vertical poles for hanging on) for the more distant ranges.

The first weekend after training began, we had liberty (time off), and I took a bus to Santa Monica to visit a couple of cousins whom my mother grew up with (her grandparents had raised them all).

While there, I borrowed a car (from another cousin in Northridge), returned to Camp Pendleton and bought a dress blue uniform. (A great way to spend the $96 a month I was now earning—I only made that much because of the four months of reserve duty I served on the 120-day delay contract and my meritorious promotion.) The drawback: I got a speeding ticket on Camp Pendleton in a borrowed car. Fortunately, the military policeman took pity on me and gave me a warning. Now I just needed to finish another week or so of ITR and then I would be off to Memphis for the beginning of my aviation training.

3

Naval Air Station, Memphis

Millington, Tennessee, Fall 1966

After ITR, we were allocated a short leave (vacation) which I spent in Moberly with my parents. The aviation contract Marines were all to proceed to Naval Air Station, Memphis, Tennessee, located in Millington, just north of Memphis, for aviation fundamentals training, known as AFam, and selection of our final MOS. While in Moberly, I learned that my cousin Patty Gunn (my mother's sister's daughter) was there and that she was married to Dick Gunn, a Navy chief, who was returning to Millington about the same time my leave was up. So I snagged a ride with them to my next duty station.

Several events occurred while waiting for our training to begin. First, we got in some serious dental work. The navy is very fond of removing wisdom teeth, and since I still had mine, they had to go.

Navy dentists, while fine physicians, can be a sadistic bunch. When I was told they were going to take my wisdom teeth out, the dentist said he would take two out at a time, and I assumed he meant on the same side and that I would still be able to chew on the other side of my mouth. Oh no, he took the upper tooth on the left side and the lower tooth on the right side, then reversed it for the other two teeth.

Fortunately, Patty took care of me while I recovered from the wisdom teeth. She provided plenty of soup and a bit of alcohol. I'm pretty sure that is where I had my first "screwdriver."

The next event that appeared on my horizon was guard duty. I spent several nights guarding an empty warehouse, not because it needed guarding but because the navy needed something for me (and others) to do while waiting for training to begin. My first general order, "To take charge of this post and all government property in sight," still rings loud in my mind.

3. Naval Air Station, Memphis

My first Thanksgiving in the Corps occurred while I was assigned to Memphis. I caught a flight out of Memphis to St. Louis and expected to catch a further flight to Moberly. Unfortunately, I was flying standby and there were no more seats available. Arrival in St. Louis was late in the evening and there were no later flights scheduled into Moberly. As luck would have it, I ran into my mother's boss, who was in St. Louis on business. He shared his hotel room with me, and I traveled the next day into Moberly via Greyhound. He stayed in St. Louis to finish his business meetings. I didn't know there were so many places for a bus to stop between St. Louis and Moberly. Fortunately, after Thanksgiving, there were plenty of seats available, and the return flights to Memphis were uneventful.

I also went into downtown Memphis one weekend and spent it with a friend of my grandfather. She was an older lady and lived next door to Elvis. While there, I got to help gather and return his peacocks, which tended to wander off. Apparently, this was a common occurrence, and she was well acquainted with the residents of the Presley mansion.

A Marine career planner, in a review of my service record book (SRB), noticed that I had a couple of years of college under my belt and suggested that I apply for the Officer Candidate Course (OCC; I was now 20 and could begin the application process). I began the procedure by sitting for the college comprehensive examination, which verified my academic level and understanding. I did not fully understand the application process, so when I completed training at Memphis and departed for my next assignment, I thought all I had to do was wait and I would soon be on the way to Officer Candidate School (OCS). In actuality, my application was in limbo since I had not completed all aspects of the process.

As the last event in my stay at Millington, I completed the AFam course. Near the completion of AFam, I was selected for air traffic controller training which would be done at Kessler Air Force Base (AFB). Normally, training for this specialty was conducted with the navy at NAS Brunswick Georgia, but the high demand for controllers in Vietnam required an additional pipeline and Kessler provided that pipeline.

I left Millington on December 2 and was attached to the Marine Aviation Detachment, NAS Pensacola, Florida, for training with the air force at Keesler AFB, Biloxi, Mississippi.

4

Keesler Air Force Base
Biloxi, Mississippi, 1966–1967

There were 60 of us sent to Keesler AFB in Biloxi, Mississippi, for training with the air force, 59 privates and privates first class and 1 corporal. The air force arranged for all the Marines to be billeted in one building located in the southwest corner of the base.

This was a big change in the way we lived from what we had been exposed to so far. At boot camp, ITR and Memphis, we were quartered either in Quonset huts or an open squad bay barracks. Here at Keesler, the air force had us in rooms, two or three Marines to a room, with a common area in each major portion of the barracks.

Training at Keesler was around the clock, in six-hour shifts. I went to "school" five days a week from 5:00 p.m. to 11:00 p.m. By the time we got back to the barracks each night, we barely had time to change clothes and head to the bars just outside the back gate.

The air force expected us to walk about a half mile north along a street beside our barracks then turn west for another half mile to get out the gate. The large grassy area just west of us happened to be the base golf course; the Pythagorean theorem would seem to indicate that it was more expedient to head straight northwest across the golf course to more efficiently maximize our available drinking time. Somehow, the air force took offense at this and attempted to prevent our trespass of the golf course. I mean, hell, nobody was playing golf after eleven in the evening, and we needed to save a little time. We met the challenge head on and kept the air force at bay; no Marine was ever captured on the golf course although there were a couple of close calls.

Our corporal was a Canadian transplant and try as he might, he had difficulty keeping us in check. Our exploits on the golf course were not the only thing the air force found frustrating about having 60 Marines among them. Occasionally we would be late leaving the bars outside the gate, and on return we would find the nearest gate locked. Rather than walk the three or four miles around the base to the front gate, we applied our obstacle course skills and climbed the fence, then proceeded across the golf course to our barracks. The air force solution to our insurrection was to integrate us into the ranks of the airmen by assigning one Marine to room with two airmen instead of being billeted together.

That didn't last long. Within a couple of weeks, the Marine Corps sent a master sergeant to take charge of us. He immediately had the air force move us back into a single barracks area where he could supervise us. With his arrival and taking charge, our behavior improved considerably. We still abused the golf course, but we weren't as obvious about it, and in return he took care of us.

I was promoted to lance corporal in late January 1967 with a date of rank of January 1. As previously stated, I didn't have a complete understanding of the process for applying to OCS, so I had convinced myself that I was going to OCS as soon as I finished at Keesler. I was able to convince the instructors at ATC school that I needed to complete the training as soon as possible to get to OCS. So I was allowed to "wash ahead"—that is, complete a two-week section of instruction by "testing out" at the end of the first week and then actually graduate one week sooner than the Marine Corps was expecting.

We had an interesting training cycle, which included classes in Federal Air Regulations, weather observation and reporting, reading and writing notice to airmen, tower procedures including the movement of aircraft on the ground to and from the runways, spotting and controlling aircraft within the airport airspace, and finally radar control of aircraft on approach and ground-controlled approach (GCA) to final landing.

The Marines completing ATC training at NAS Brunswick, Georgia, had to take the civilian ATC competency test, but the air force did not require that of their controllers. So we had an extra session at Keesler where we were administered the test. I completed my civilian requirements for certification with ease. (Perhaps I was learning to study.)

Upon completion of the standardized test and air force training as an air traffic controller, I had orders to Marine Corps Air Station, Beaufort, South Carolina, with a brand-new MOS—6713, Air Traffic Controlman, Radar.

The Marine Corps did not expect me to be ready for transfer for another week, so I had to remain at Keesler and reside in the barracks until my scheduled departure date. I learned later that it was not uncommon for Headquarters Marine Corps to be a little behind the power curve when issuing orders. When I finally executed my orders, I was assigned to Marine Air Traffic Control Unit (MATCU) 69, Marine Air Base Squadron (MABS) 31, Marine Aircraft Group (MAG) 31, Second Marine Air Wing (2ndMAW), Marine Corps Air Station (MCAS), Beaufort, South Carolina.

I had a brief leave period between Keesler and Beaufort, so I returned home for a visit. While there, I went to Kansas to visit the girlfriend I had throughout the last two years of school. Since I had no car and was too young to rent one, I borrowed Mom and Dad's for the trip. My girlfriend was in a Catholic girls' school near Lawrence, Kansas. For the two-day trip, she had made reservations for me at a nearby hotel. The first night there, we attended a formal dance (I wore my blues). I don't think I was much of a date as I was tired from the drive and had trouble staying awake during the well-lit affair. The next morning, I picked her up for an early breakfast, and after returning her to the school, I returned to Moberly.

Soon after that, I was on the way to MCAS Beaufort, South Carolina.

5

Marine Corps Air Station
Beaufort, South Carolina, 1967

MCAS Beaufort was a noisy place, with MAG-31 and its five squadrons of F-4, twin engine jet fighters assigned there. It's been said that the F-4 is proof positive that if you put a big enough engine on a brick, it will fly. Doesn't matter. I thought they were beautiful aircraft, carrying death and destruction to the enemy. Arriving there in mid–April, it was starting to warm up. The bugs were coming out and I was so glad I went to boot camp on the West Coast. MCRD Parris Island was only a few miles away through the swamp and coastal muck from the air station. I was already looking forward to the end of May when the base pool would open.

MATCU-69 was commanded by a limited duty officer, who was a second lieutenant mustang. Marine officers who were formerly enlisted were referred to as mustangs. The unit was on the north side of the airfield; our barracks and the mess hall were on the south side. In fact, everything we needed, other than our worksite, was on the south side: quarters, mess hall, base theater, chapel, bowling alley, Marine Corps exchange, enlisted club, MAG-31 and MABS-31 headquarters.

The officers' club and bachelor officer quarters (BOQ) were about two-thirds of the way around the airfield, but we (young, enlisted Marines) didn't need to go there. With all the base facilities on the south side of the airfield, bus service was not considered necessary. From our barracks to the worksite was about a three-mile hike, not a big deal for a new Marine but not something I was looking forward to on a four-times-a-day basis (once to work, once to chow and back to work and, finally after work, back to our quarters). The senior NCOs (SNCOs) and our officer in charge (OIC) all had cars, but there weren't enough of them to give everybody a ride. So walk we must.

Now back with the Marine Corps and back to barracks-style living.

The young men of MATCU-69 lived on the second story of the barracks in an open squad bay configuration. The only privacy was our wall lockers laid out to form cubicles so that each cubical housed four to six of us.

A few of the newly qualified controllers were assigned to the air station ATC system for local certification. The rest of us went on the daily hike to MATCU-69 where we trained on deployable equipment. The deployable GCA units rarely worked properly as all parts for that equipment were prioritized to Vietnam. We also participated in normal Marine training activities, like running, preparing for inspections and the quarterly physical fitness test.

During this time, I learned that every unit admin clerk has previously applied and been turned down for every program the Marine Corps offers. It is important not to be affected by their negativity and to pursue your own dreams despite their negative opinions about your chances. So after being told that there was no chance that I would ever be selected, I completed (properly) and submitted my application for OCS.

I had a great deal of respect for my OIC at MATCU, and apparently, he thought my work ethic and Marine traits were noteworthy since I earned a meritorious promotion to corporal and received an excellent recommendation on my application for OCS. I was promoted on June 16 with a date of rank of June 1, 1966.

Occasionally we had unit parties. There was a fund created out of profits generated at the Marine Corps exchange that paid for beer and fixings. Fixings were usually large hunks of meat (called steaks) that we grilled on old oil drums that had been bisected and filled with charcoal. Our unit gunnery sergeant was responsible for picking up the liquid we were going to consume. His favorite was Carling Black Label, which

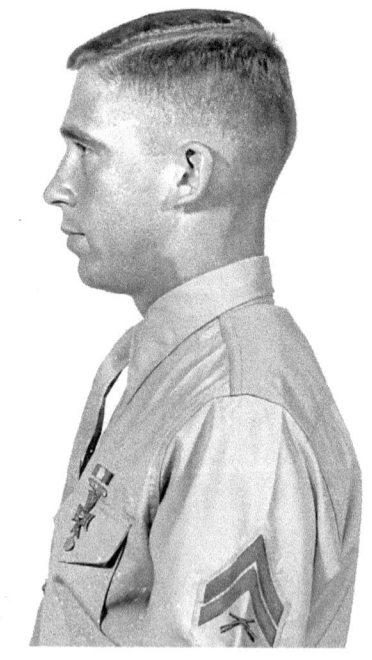

My OCS application photograph.

5. Marine Corps Air Station

he bought a lot of, and some variety of soda, which he bought little of. I was not a beer fan, and I didn't think that Carling Black Label was a "good" beer, but there wasn't much soda, so I participated.

During the summer, I went back to Moberly on leave, and while there, I bought a bright red 1967 Camaro Rally Sport with a 327 cubic inch engine. It cost me $2,000 including tax and license. This was going to make my daily trip to MATCU a lot easier (and me a lot more popular).

Once back at MCAS Beaufort with a car, our (my friends' and my) horizons were expanded. Early in the fall I got a "Dear John" letter from the longtime girlfriend I had visited while home in April. Can't say that I was a great boyfriend, but it hit me very hard. I participated in a good night of drinking at the NCO club doing shots of vodka with a water chaser. Eventually I was chugging the vodka and looking at the water for a chaser.

The NCO club had a long, canopied walk from the front door to the street. When the evening was done, I walked to the end of the canopy and leaned against one of the posts holding the canopy up, while waiting for my friend to pick me up. As he arrived with the car, my feet slid out from under me, and I slid down the pole, landing on my butt. My friend loaded me up, hauled me to the barracks where I spent the night lying in the shower throwing up massive amounts of alcohol.

After a couple of days of recovery, my friends and I began a series of forays to Georgia Southern College (now University) in Statesboro, in search of female companionship. I met a nice young lady there and saw her on every trip back to Statesboro. Later I would return to Savannah for flight school and saw her many times while there.

While at Beaufort, I was screened for and received my first security clearance. I was granted a secret clearance, then I was assigned to "reliability training." I had no idea what this was about before arriving at the classroom. There, we (there were just a few of us) were told that we were being screened to guard some "special" weapons that were being brought here for training with the F-4 crews. As it turned out, I never had to stand that guard duty, but I was called on in later years to receive additional training as an aircrew member for the transportation (not delivery) of those weapons.

My application for OCS was slowly working its way through the approval process. Since I was applying from an aviation unit, my career planner had me take some aviation qualification exams and a flight physical (medical examination to qualify for duty involving flight in and control of aircraft). I did well on the written exams and passed the physical.

A military flight physical is not like going to the doctor. The military does everything in groups and applies the "hurry up and wait" technique. Flight physicals are no different. Everyone scheduled for a flight physical showed up at the same time (usually around 0700). The corpsmen (enlisted assistants to the doctors similar to physician's assistants) were present but usually drinking coffee and preparing for the day's activities.

The assembled victims of this medical malpractice were sitting and waiting until about 0730, when the actual physicals would begin. The collective group would begin with updating medical histories, then were divided into subgroups and sent various directions to complete preliminary events such as blood draws, eyesight exams, hearing tests, and chest X-rays. Each event would involve additional waiting while each individual in the group completed the task. Eventually everyone's final stop was with the doctor who conducted chest and stomach palpations, hernia and prostate exams.

Physicals were generally complete by noon. Throughout my 25-year career, flight physicals were conducted in the same manner, with the only difference being the number of people in the group.

I assumed (and was encouraged to believe) that since I was wearing glasses at the time that upon completion of OCS (if selected), I would be sent directly to flight school to qualify as a radar intercept officer (RIO) in the F-4 aircraft. The RIO sits in the back seat of the F-4 and uses the internal weapons systems to assist the pilot and is not required to have 20–20 vision. I would have a very pleasant surprise later.

Multiple trips to Georgia Southern during the fall ensued. During the off payday weekends, we stopped at a backdoor business in Beaufort to purchase some wine, really good stuff. We were able to buy a case for $5, allocated $10 for gas and $20 for a motel, so for $35 split between four guys, we could have a great weekend (we didn't eat much on these weekends, but we did have some horrendous hangovers!).

Downtown Beaufort had a fast-food pioneer in a place called Burger Queen, which we frequented. The base bowling alley also had a great little grill when we didn't want to use the mess hall or were late getting back from MATCU, which was frequent.

In September, I qualified for consideration for promotion to sergeant, but I missed the cutting score by two points. Cutting scores were determined by a complex mixture of events, each assigned a point value, which included "time in grade," "time in service," rifle and/or pistol qualification, physical fitness test scores and "proficiency and conduct marks." The required score for promotion was 130, and I had a booming 128. I think cutting scores now exist in the four-digit category.

5. Marine Corps Air Station

In December, I planned a trip home for Christmas, offering seats in the Camaro to three other Missouri residents who would share the cost of gas. I got home a few days before Christmas and was enjoying a good visit with my family when I got a call from my non-commissioned officer-in-charge (NCOIC), a master gunnery sergeant, who said my leave was being cut short. My application for OCS had been approved and I was to report to Quantico, Virginia, on January 2, 1968. I needed to get back early so I could complete the checkout procedures prior to transferring to Quantico. Luckily, I had the phone numbers for the other Marines I had dropped in St. Louis, so I called the guys to advise them of my revised travel plan. They elected to stay to the end of their normal leave and would find their own way back.

I left home on the 26th and drove straight through to Beaufort. I got checked out by the 29th and left with another OCS selectee," Bob, who was a resident of New York, for his home. We planned to spend New Year's Eve at his home, then head back to Quantico.

Before embarking on this adventure, I met with my OIC, and he gave me his gold bars to use for my commissioning. My friend and I headed to New York, arriving on the 30th. We spent New Year's Eve cruising the bars and making new friends. We elected not to go into downtown New York City, figuring it wasn't going to be worth the hassle. We left New York the morning of the 2nd after a brief hangover recovery period and reported in at Quantico late that night. OCS would begin in earnest in the morning.

6

OCS, Marine Corps Base

Quantico, Virginia, 1968

If you are ever privileged enough to drive through Mainside, MCB Quantico, continue past the airfield on the left where HMX-1 lives, then past the former home of the FBI training facility on the right and continue to the back remote corner.

That's where OCS is held. My friend Bob and I reported there on January 2, 1968. We also met up with another OCS selectee from Beaufort, Tim. Bob and I ended up assigned to Second Platoon, 49th OCC. Tim was in Third Platoon, but I didn't have contact with him again until after OCS was complete. Tim completed OCS successfully and I saw him frequently in TBS. Bob suffered an injury in OCS and returned to MCAS Beaufort to finish his enlistment.

I'd been to Marine boot camp and survived. There couldn't be anything worse, could there? Many times, I've been asked the difference between boot camp and OCS. They are very similar and yet very different.

In both, the DIs (boot camp) and the sergeant instructors (OCS) are intent on weeding out those people who are not Marine or Marine officer material. In both, the physical training was intense. The difference—in boot camp, we never knew our schedule, when we would be subjected to physical fitness drills or any other planned activity until told by our DI; in OCS, every minute was planned out, we had a complete schedule and we knew when we would train at what activity and for how long.

We knew the length of each hike and run and what our performance was expected to be. In boot camp, if you weren't cutting it but the DIs thought you could, you were sent back to another platoon that wasn't as far along in training; the same for OCS. If the DIs in boot camp thought you were hopeless, you were sent home; in OCS, if you weren't officer material, you were sent back to MCRD Parris Island to see if you could cut it as a Marine enlisted man.

In boot camp, the emphasis was on teamwork and instant obedience to orders; in OCS, it was teamwork and leadership skills and style. In boot camp, our trainers were DIs and were addressed as "sir"; in fact, every sentence that we spoke started and ended with "sir." In OCS, our instructors were "sergeant instructor," and we caught hell if we ever addressed them as "sir."

As we progressed through training, leadership problem-solving events were added to the end of stressful physical training events. In the brutal cold of January and early February mornings in Quantico, a long (five or more miles) hike along the frozen, slippery slopes of the Potomac River was followed by an immediate problem-solving exercise where one of us tackled the problem and led three or four others through the drill.

These events were very challenging. In most cases, there was no solution; the exercise was designed to test our leadership skills, to see the innovative attempts at finding a solution and to see how we employed those under our direction. The hikes preceding these exercises included wearing full combat gear. In fact, except for some specific physical exercises, everything we did in OCS was in full combat gear. It wasn't long until my January 2 reporting weight of 175 pounds was back to the 150 the Marine Corps thought I should weigh.

One of the big physical challenges in OCS was the obstacle course. It consisted of seven events that you climbed over, jumped over or ran through and mostly survived. It always finished with a sprint back to the beginning point. I ran track and played football in high school. My body type was not the big bruiser; I was mostly a moderately skinny, wiry type with significant upper-body strength. As a sophomore in high school, I completed a 20-foot hand-over-hand rope climb in 4.5 seconds. The "O" course was my forte. We were also introduced to the double running of the "O" course, which is where after sprinting back to the starting point you continued through the course a second time. I might have been the only "officer candidate" who preferred the obstacle course to any of our other training events.

We lived in an open squad bay at OCS, more like boot camp than any other experience I had encountered so far. There was no separation in living areas, just rows of two-tiered racks with footlockers and wall lockers between them.

On each Friday night, we conducted a field day (thorough cleaning and polishing) in our barracks including weapon and uniform cleaning. Saturday mornings, we had an inspection, and after the second week, if we passed, we could have weekend liberty. Since I had significant experience cleaning my weapon and preparing a uniform for inspection, I knew it would be easier for me to prepare after everybody else was out of the way. After the field day, I would go to the "candidate's club" across the street from our barracks and have a drink or two and listen to music. My favorite song, "Love Is Blue" by Paul Mauriat, was released that January. Perhaps I was still a bit nostalgic about the girlfriend who dumped me in the middle of last year. I still stop and listen anytime I hear it being played. After taps, I would return to the squad bay and do my prep for the next day's inspection.

On Saturday afternoons, my bunkmate and I would journey to D.C. in pursuit of companionship. He had friends attending an all-female Catholic school in the heart of D.C., so we generally had a good time, although that good time was usually just a nice dinner in Georgetown with a few drinks, then returning the ladies to their college.

Near the end of OCS, we had a field meet in which the three platoons in each of the two companies that would graduate together competed against each other in several events including an "O" course competition, a three-mile run and other physical exercises that we had practiced many times. The four-man team from my platoon (including myself) set an "O" course record that stood for many years.

I had become eligible for promotion to sergeant while in OCS but missed the cutting score again. The new cutting score—133; mine, 131. I often joke with friends that I couldn't make sergeant, so the Marine Corps made me a second lieutenant.

The first week in March, we graduated from OCS and were commissioned second lieutenants in the Marine Corps. Initially, we were assigned a date of rank of January 1, 1966, the same as that year's graduating class from the Naval Academy. Years later, that was amended to March 8, our graduation date. After graduation and commissioning, I had orders to Basic School, which was a bit of a surprise since I thought I was going straight to "flight school." I later learned that the straight-to-flight school path ended with the 48th OCC. A few of my friends (whom I met later) were in that group, and those who went straight to army flight training were still second lieutenants when they got to Vietnam.

My parents and two friends of theirs flew out for the ceremony. After the ceremony, I had to move from the OCS barracks to the BOQ

Opposite top: **My mother pinning on my bars as a second lieutenant. My dad is to her left.** *Opposite bottom:* **My dad and I packing my red Camaro for the move to TBS.**

6. OCS, Marine Corps Base

at TBS deeper in the interior of MCB Quantico. To accomplish this, we had the five of us and all my gear wedged in my '67 Camaro. After moving into the BOQ, the five of us did a weekend tour of D.C. and all its wonderful sights. Afterward, Mom, Dad, and their friends flew on to New York, continuing their vacation before returning to Missouri.

7

The Basic School, MCB

Quantico, Virginia, Summer 1968

When referring to The Basic School, "the" was always emphasized, so it was abbreviated "TBS" instead of just "BS." There must have been some thought put into this—just not sure what it was or what image they wanted to project or protect.

At TBS, we lived and were treated like the officers we had become. We were quartered two to a BOQ room, with real wall lockers to store our personal belongings as well as our military gear. Like previous evolutions, we kept our rifles locked to our racks so we would have them available for training each day instead of having to draw them from the armory. Like boot camp, we trained with the "M-14," a great rifle, chambered in 7.62 mm, as opposed to the newer "M-16" which was being introduced. The "M-14" is a heavy, long-barreled weapon accurate at great distance. The "M-16" is much lighter and short-barreled, chambered in the NATO standard 5.56 mm and more useful in the close jungle environs of Vietnam.

From the first week in March until the first week in August, we had a broader version of ITR. We had weeks of intensive classroom instruction and field drills on every facet of what a Marine infantry officer had to know and do. This was part of the Marine creed: Every Marine is a rifleman! In the case of officers, every Marine officer can lead a rifle platoon in combat.

Through our time at TBS, we studied individual military skills and various elements of support to the ground component. Each day of classroom instruction was followed by two or three days of fieldwork that exercised and emphasized that element of instruction. Military skills training included land navigation, map reading, rifle and pistol qualification, calls for fire and unarmed combat. Our support training would include the use of artillery, tanks, amphibious tractors (known as amtracs), air support, the weapons company, shipboard and amphibious assault operations.

Classroom work began with instruction on the elements of a squad (three fire teams and a squad leader), a platoon (three squads, a radioman, a platoon sergeant and a platoon leader), a company (three platoons, a radioman, a company gunny, a company executive officer (XO) and a commanding officer), a battalion (three infantry companies, a weapons company, a radioman, a battalion sergeant major, a battalion staff, an XO and a commanding officer), a regiment (three Battalions, a staff and a commanding officer) and a division (three infantry regiments, an artillery regiment, tanks and amtracs, a staff and a commanding general). By now, you've noticed some similarities—each unit consists of three subordinate units and the appropriate supplemental staff.

The aviation side of the Marine Corps is a little different and is more task organized. Normally, the smallest basic unit is the squadron and is equivalent to a battalion. The squadron can break down into smaller detachments consisting of two or more aircraft. The group matches with a regiment and the wing matches the division. Classroom work on structure was followed by fieldwork on fire team, squad and platoon tactics.

As TBS proceeded, Quantico's freezing weather of January, February and March had transitioned to the dry, dusty, blistering heat of summer in Virginia.

At TBS, our BOQ had a dining room and a separate bar in the building. This portion of Marine Corps Base Quantico spanned two counties and the county line ran through the bar in the BOQ. As luck would have it, one of the counties was "dry" and the other permitted alcohol sales. The serving area in the bar was in the county that permitted alcohol sales, so we could only buy our drinks in that part of the bar, then we could carry them to a table in the dry portion. The bartender could not serve us in the dry part of the bar.

Our class had five companies of between 40 and 50 second lieutenants each. TBS had an a cappella choral group that performed at the "Mess Night" that each class held just prior to graduation. I tried out and was selected to participate in the group, so I got to attend several "Mess Nights" prior to our own.

One day while walking to the BOQ, I observed another second lieutenant fail to return the salute of an enlisted Marine who had rendered honors as they passed. I immediately stopped the lieutenant and

7. The Basic School, MCB

corrected that behavior. He was also a new second lieutenant; however, neither of us knew who was senior. We just behaved as if it were me.

Like OCS, each Saturday morning, we had a room and uniform inspection, and if we did well, we had liberty until Sunday night. My bunk mate from OCS and I continued our forays into Washington seeking female companionship and expanded our trips to Mary Washington College in Fredericksburg.

The weekend before we qualified on the rifle range, we met a coed at Mary Washington College (now University), drove about halfway into D.C. to pick up her roommate, then decided to continue into Georgetown for a few late drinks. At that time, Mary Washington was an all-girls school, so finding a date was not difficult. As it turned out, that weekend there were race riots in D.C.; all access to the area was blocked off. We had to turn around at the K Street bridge and head back. After about four hours of driving, we had dropped the ladies off at Mary Washington and were back at the BOQ, without dinner, drinks or kisses!

The next weekend, I was supposed to have a second date with the same girl. However, she had suffered a severe sunburn the day before and was unable to join me. I didn't find this out until I got to Mary Washington to pick her up. When I arrived, the student on duty at the dormitory desk told me about the sunburn, then introduced me to a friend of hers, Caroline. I went out with Caroline that night and again on every weekend that I was not involved in training. Seemed like a positive thing was developing. She graduated in May, and I didn't get to see her again till late July, when I was able to visit her in Maryland.

Before I left MATCU-69, one of my friends had invited me to his wedding in Brooklyn which was to be held this summer. As it worked out, I had that weekend off, so I drove to New York Friday night, spent the weekend with his family and helped him celebrate his wedding. I went out to Long Island on Saturday with a cousin of his and then attended the wedding on Sunday. Sunday night was a very long drive back to Quantico but well worth it. As a young corporal, he kept marveling that "there is an officer at my wedding." I was glad to be there, and he should be celebrating his 59th anniversary by now!

There was a warrant officer class going through training while we were in TBS. Unlike the army, the Marines select senior sergeants and staff sergeants for designation as a warrant officer. Since I had a lot in common with them, I spent considerable time on the BOQ bar conducting social activities with them.

In July, my brother Bob flew out to spend a weekend; he was about to start his junior year at Culver Stockton College in Canton, Missouri, just north of Hannibal. He came in on a Friday while I was participating in a field exercise. Fortunately, one of my friends, who was on limited duty due to an injury, was able to pick him up. My friend before attending OCS and TBS had been a defensive end for the Dallas Cowboys.

My brother and I decided to swing by Mary Washington to see if we could score a date for a Saturday night dinner in Georgetown. That attempt was successful, and we had a great evening of steaks, wine and company. We dropped the girls off back in Fredericksburg very late (early morning), returned to Quantico and managed to get some sleep before I had to drop him at Washington National for his flight back to Missouri.

During the course of TBS, we would participate in a four-day amphibious assault on the beaches of Little Creek, Virginia, utilizing a navy amphibious assault vessel (known in the fleet as an "amphib") and landing craft and later conduct a three-day war where several of us would rotate through the role of company commander. I didn't know it then, but during later deployments on amphibs, I came to realize that the ship we were on was one of the filthiest ships in the navy. It was very poorly maintained.

During my turn as the "company commander" in the three-day war, I called for an "arc light" (a B-52 bombing sortie) when we walked into the first ambush. Our instructors were impressed but thought it was overkill. I worked down the list of potential support vehicles, finally getting approval for mortar and machine gun support.

Midway through our training, we listed our top three choices for our final MOS. The higher your class standing, the more likely you would get one of your choices. My top choice was flight school.

The top military skills student would be awarded an M1911, a .45-caliber semiautomatic pistol. I did very well in all the skills, qualified "expert" with the rifle and pistol but bombed the paper test on artillery and missed winning the pistol by one-tenth of a GPA point.

Those of us who were opting for flight training (either as a pilot or RIO) would also have to take another flight physical to ensure we were still qualified. Near the end of TBS, potential flight selectees were sent to MCAS Quantico for flight physicals. I had worn glasses throughout high school, junior college (now known as community college) and while serving as an enlisted Marine as a result of an astigmatism. As I aged, my glasses requirement changed; during my final flight physical, my eyesight tested 20/20, so I was able to qualify for pilot training.

The top 20 aviation qualified personnel in our TBS class were assigned for training to the air force with an ultimate assignment in jet fighters. The next 20 (including me) were assigned for training to the army at Ft. Wolters, Texas, for qualification in helicopters. The last 20 went to Pensacola, Florida, for training with the navy. Some of this last group would end up in helicopters, the rest in either jets or KC-130s.

TBS wrapped up in early August, and I didn't have to be at Ft. Wolters until the 19th. So I had a few days of leave to use before reporting.

One of my best friends through TBS was of Japanese descent; his parents and grandparents had been interned in a camp in California during World War II. He attended Washington State University for his undergraduate degree. His parents and grandparents spoke Japanese at home, but he couldn't speak a word of it; in fact, when he took Japanese as his language option, he failed it. Every December 7, members of his fraternity would capture him, strip him naked and throw him in a snowbank.

He and I decided to room together in flight school and would meet at the airport in Ft. Worth on August 18. I drove from Quantico on I-70 to Missouri; he took the southern route driving straight to Texas where he would leave his car in airport parking, flying on to his home in Monrovia, California.

8

U.S. Army Primary Flight Training

Ft. Wolters, Texas, Fall 1968

Ft. Wolters is located in Mineral Wells, Texas, about 40 miles west of Ft. Worth along I-20/US 30. Texas in the fall was hot. It stayed warm enough to go swimming even in December when our training here was complete.

Of the 20 of us assigned to the army, 10 were required to report within two weeks of finishing TBS, the second 10 came in two weeks later. My Japanese friend Hank and I reported together on August 19, 1968.

Upon arriving in Ft. Worth and before reporting to Ft. Wolters, Hank and I did a quick search for an apartment and found a nice place just south of the interstate and east of Carswell AFB. Hank and I went to Denny's for lunch during our apartment search, and I ended up with a date for later in the evening with a waitress. This was a good sign for things to come in Texas.

Several of the army students also rented apartments in the Ft. Worth area before we were told we had to live within a few miles of Mineral Wells. That didn't bother us much; we stayed in Ft. Worth anyway! There was a lot more to do there than in Mineral Wells, and the complex Hank and I were in had a pool.

Marines in flight training with the army were considered to be in a temporary additional duty (TAD) status and were paid an additional $20 a day for billeting and meals. Years later, I realized that TAD status really meant "traveling around drunk."

I still had my Camaro, and Hank had an MGB Spider. Two army students and Hank and I carpooled from Ft. Worth to Ft. Wolters each day. Between the four of us, only two had cars large enough to fit all of

8. U.S. Army Primary Flight Training

us, so when it was Hank's turn to drive, he drove my Camaro and the rest of us caught up on our sleep.

Our flight class had our ten Marines; about 40-some commissioned soldiers, a class of warrant officer candidates (also about 40) and several Vietnamese army students (who had undergone English-language instruction prior to being assigned to flight training). The warrant officer candidates lived in a barracks and were essentially in boot camp while undergoing flight training. Unlike the Marine Corps, the army commissions warrant officers without any previous enlisted service. Army warrant officers were usually right out of high school and showed some aviation potential.

Our first two weeks at Ft. Wolters consisted of classroom instruction. The academics included theory of flight, helicopter aerodynamics, weather, navigation and map reading. Map reading at 100 knots is significantly different than standing on a hill and orienting yourself to your surroundings. We also met the civilian contractors who would be our flight instructors.

To differentiate between various classes and the stage of training they were involved in, the army issued us colored baseball hats. The class I was in wore white hats; another friend told me his class wore gray hats.

Initial flight instruction was in the TH-55, an aircraft manufactured by the Howard Hughes Aircraft Company. It was a two-seater with a four-cylinder reciprocating gas engine and minimal instrumentation (an attitude indicator, airspeed indicator, altimeter, a radio compass, a vertical speed indicator, rate-of-turn indicator and some basic engine instrumentation). The connection between the engine and transmission was an 8 V-belt fan belt assembly with an electric tension adjustment. Our flight instructors were civilian contract instructors, provided by Southern Airways, a Texas company. Each instructor was assigned two or three students. The students would pre-flight the aircraft together, then the instructor and one student would fly to an outlying field for our training. The other students rode a bus and waited their turn for instruction. While we waited our turn to fly, we were able to watch the Summer Olympics of 1968 on a TV in the waiting area.

A different student would fly back to the main airfield each day with the instructor and conduct a post-flight inspection, while the others rode the bus. The bus ride was about 50 minutes, while the flight to and from the training area was about 15 or 20 minutes.

Initial flight instruction consisted of takeoffs, climb to altitude, cruise to the training area, autorotations (in case of engine failure), descent and landing, hover work and inflight emergency procedures.

Hover work was the first thing we were required to obtain proficiency in, then autorotations.

There is a distinct difference between an inflight autorotation and a hovering autorotation, and that difference can lead to disastrous consequences. Inflight engine failure requires that the collective (the control that makes the aircraft go up and down by controlling the pitch of the rotor blades) be immediately and firmly pushed to its bottom stop. Without that action, the pitch on the rotor blades will cause the rotor blades to slow to the point that they will stop, and the aircraft will descend like a glass dropped off a table with the same result at the bottom!

A hovering autorotation, however, requires that the collective be held momentarily, then gradually pulled up to increase pitch on the blades, which increases lift and allows a gentle descent of the aircraft to the ground as the rotor blades slow. In my second or third hour of instruction and after practicing several inflight autorotations, my instructor introduced an engine failure while hovering.

I immediately and forcefully bottomed the collective, which resulted in the aircraft striking the ground very hard, bending the skids and cross tubes and damaging the bottom of the aircraft. In 23 years of flying, this was the only pilot error accident I was involved in; however, this one was credited to my instructor who failed to properly supervise my actions.

While flying to and from our training area, initially I had moderate difficulty establishing a proper instrument scan, thus allowing the aircraft to drift off the recommended tolerances of speed, altitude and heading. My instructor, who was a screamer, got so frustrated that while knocking on the altimeter with his knuckle, he broke the glass facing on the instrument. Coupled with his failure to supervise my autorotation, his supervisors thought his temperament might need adjusting, so he was given a break from instruction and then reassigned to different students. I got a new instructor who had a much smoother temperament.

As our training progressed, we were expected to "solo"—that is, conduct a flight without an instructor in the aircraft at between 8 and 13 hours of instruction. We were approaching the eight-hour mark at the end of our second week of flying. The ten Marines in our flight class each contributed a quart bottle of our favorite booze to form a pool that would be the prize for the first one of us to fly "solo."

Each Friday, we adjourned to the officers' club for a little libation before returning to Ft. Worth. The Friday at the end of our second week of flying, we encountered an army officer who was bragging about and willing to "take on" all comers in a one-armed push-up contest. Marines, being extremely competitive, rarely resist a challenge, so I willingly entered the competition. The young soldier knocked out four or five good one-arm push-ups; I continued through that point and finished with about 15, easily winning the contest. Unfortunately, I injured my shoulder during the quest and was medically grounded from flight for the next week.

When I returned to flight status, the other Marines in my class had all completed their solo flight. My instructor acknowledged that I was falling behind my classmates and decided that I should solo after a brief warm-up flight. Although all of the Marines had their solo flight from one to three days before I did, when I soloed, I had less total flight time than they did. Thus, when I got my solo flight, I was the first to solo based on flight time in the aircraft and was awarded the accumulated booze prize.

After our solos, much of our flight training centered on continued practice on approaches and landings, practice autorotations, and solo navigation. After an initial introduction in technique by our instructors, we practiced confined area and pinnacle landings solo. We spent many hours trying smaller and smaller confined areas, then returning to the landing pattern for more practice approaches and autorotations.

Sometime in September or October, Hank and I, the two army officers whom we carpooled with and a few other Marine friends went to an after-hours club in Dallas. While there, one of my friends started a flirtatious conversation with a young lady whose date seemed to take offense. A challenge was issued, and we all headed outside to settle our differences. As we cleared the door, I realized that the Texas native had pulled a gun. I grabbed Hank by the shirt collar and pulled him back inside while screaming at the bouncer, "He's got a gun!" The bouncer pulled the biggest handgun I'd ever seen (the "Dirty Harry" movies had not come out yet) and headed out. We found another way out, got in our cars and left. The next day, I went to a gun store and bought a .32-caliber revolver and kept it in my glove compartment hoping I would never need it for personal protection. I ended up selling the weapon several years later.

In late October, all the Marines in training at Ft. Wolters organized a Marine birthday celebration complete with cake cutting to be held in Mineral Wells on November 10. Most of us were able to find dates among the Texas beauties that lived in the area, and a grand celebration was enjoyed by all in evening dresses and dress blues!

Around Thanksgiving, someone "borrowed" my Camaro for an evening. I noticed the next morning that it wasn't in the parking space where I'd left it. The police found it several hours later, several streets over. The revolver was still in the locked glove box, but my eight-track tapes had been rifled through although none were missing. I guess it was just a required joy ride; still, I was thankful to have the car back.

Near the end of our basic flight training, we were introduced to cross-country flight and navigation. We had several round robin flights with an instructor in the aircraft. He helped us organize our route and aided us while we developed a keen understanding of fuel planning and usage.

Our last solo flight prior to graduation was a long cross-country flight that stretched fuel consumption to its limit and required significant navigation planning and execution. As I was nearing the end of my cross-country flight, I could see an aircraft ahead of me that was about to enter the landing pattern. It was trailing smoke and appeared to be on fire. Several radio calls were made from the tower controller to the aircraft advising them of the apparent fire in the aircraft. The only acknowledgment from the aircraft was "roger" as the Vietnamese pilot continued to fly. He did land successfully, but before he was allowed to continue flight training, he was sent back to language school for some additional training. That was a flight where his lack of language skills could have had a disastrous outcome.

Overall, I really enjoyed Ft. Wolters but was glad to be moving on. We graduated from basic flight training on December 20, 1968, and after a short Christmas leave, we would begin advanced flight training at Hunter Army Airfield, Savannah, Georgia.

Hank and I drove back to Moberly in caravan. He spent a few days there with me, then flew back to his home in Monrovia, California, for Christmas. He would return after the New Year, and we would drive in caravan to Savannah, Georgia.

While home, I wrecked my Camaro when a friend whom I went to high school with, traveling in the oncoming lanes, turned left in front of me on an ice-covered street. I was unable to stop. To get to Savannah, I borrowed my younger brother's nearly identical Camaro for the drive. He was on probation at his college for having too much fun the previous semester, so he was not allowed to have a car on campus during the spring of 1969.

9

Advanced Flight Training, Hunter Army Airfield and Ft. Stewart

Savannah, Georgia, Early 1969

The army, in their infinite wisdom, thought they could save the Marine Corps a little money on the cost of TAD for the Marine flight students. This was done by building a short (just over a quarter mile) road that at one end was just behind the officers' club and at the other end was just inside the gate to Hunter Army Airfield. On both sides of the road, they put trailers that had two bedrooms, a kitchen and a living room. The end of the road by the "O Club" had a large turnaround. They assigned two Marines to each trailer for housing. When Hank and I checked in, there were a couple of classes already living in the trailers, and during the next several weeks, more classes/groups of Marines moved in.

Having been on per diem for the four months prior to checking in to Hunter, this quarter-mile strip next to a quality liquor source looked like a cover shot for a magazine featuring American muscle cars. Our group of bachelors took advantage of the location, most evenings and every weekend with quarter-mile matchups featuring Corvettes, Camaros, Mustangs and Thunderbirds! Friday nights after "Happy Hour" was not the best time for this diversion, but it happened anyway. We happily named this menagerie "The Zoo."

In Savannah, I was back in familiar territory from my previous tour at nearby MCAS Beaufort, South Carolina. I introduced Hank to Georgia Southern College and its collection of coeds. If we weren't racing behind the club, we were on the road to Statesboro. Many Friday nights, we would pick up our friends at Georgia Southern and bring them back to Hunter for the weekend. I had learned to cook in the Boy Scouts and had some additional specialized training from my grandmother. Many weekends, I fixed fried chicken with mashed potatoes and gravy, creamed corn and a salad with homemade Thousand Island dressing for the four of us (Hank and I and our female friends from Georgia Southern).

Our antics behind the club were finally more trouble to the army than it was worth, and with a little persuasion from a senior Marine representative from Pensacola we were allowed to move off the strip. Most of us joined forces and moved to beach houses on Savannah Beach aboard Tybee Island. It was only a 21-mile drive from the beach to the base—piece of cake for those of us who were used to the 40 miles from Ft. Worth to Ft. Wolters. The army then moved married army warrant officers into the trailers. The race strip was now shut down, but we still started our weekends at the irresistibly convenient O club.

One weekend in early February, I drove my brother's Camaro to Atlanta to meet my parents, who were returning my recently repaired car to me. It was a great but short visit. I was glad to get my own car back.

Our flight training at Hunter began with basic instrument training in the OH-13, a two-bladed Bell product with a tail that looked like it was made from scaffolding. That period of training was all dual pilot with an instructor pilot. Even though the weather was good, the entire first third of our training was spent wearing a hood over our helmets that prevented us from seeing outside the aircraft, only allowing us to see the instruments in the aircraft. This training did not get us an "instrument rating"; it only prepared us for inadvertent flight into weather conditions that prevented visual flight. Army pilots at that time did not get "instrument rated" until much later in their career. I don't recall any experiences of note during instrument training; the gauges all seemed to stay in the "green" and the engines kept running.

Back in 1969, we had not yet combined Washington's and Lincoln's Birthday holidays into President's Day. One of those provided us with a long weekend in February, so I planned to fly back to Washington, D.C., to see my friend from Mary Washington. She had graduated while I was still in Basic School, and I missed her. I was thinking that there was some potential for something permanent there. I was able to get a flight there but could not get a reservation back and I could not afford to miss a flight training day. I chose not to go and never saw her again.

Instead, I caught an advertising flight to Bermuda for two free days and nights there. The only catch was on the third day, we (everybody on the flight) had to view some property in Florida as part of a sales promotion.

9. Advanced Flight Training

The officers in my flight school class, Hunter Army Airfield, Savannah.

In the middle third of our stay at Hunter, we flew the OH-23, another two-bladed aircraft where the cockpit looked like a giant bubble and the area aft of the engine had a long, skinny boom supporting the tail rotor. In this aircraft, we were introduced to formation flight and continued training in confined-area landings. Each phase of training featured larger and more powerful/complicated aircraft.

In March 1969, I received information that I had been promoted to first lieutenant. That was a pleasant surprise pick-me-up for my paycheck. As a second lieutenant, I had been making a grand old $350.00 per month.

The last third of our training, we were introduced to the "C," "D" and "H" models of the UH-1, Iroquois. The Huey, as it was called, was the workhorse of the U.S. Army! The "C" model was used as a gunship, and the "D" and "H" models were for troop transport, resupply and medevac. After a short qualification syllabus in the Huey, we had a little bit of gunship instruction, then formation and confined-area landings for that type/model aircraft. Most of our flying over the last month or so consisted of formation flight and confined-area landings. Most of our flying was done either solo (with a crew chief) or dual pilot with another student.

In April, during spring break for Georgia Southern, I went to Swainsboro to meet my Georgia girlfriend's parents. This was another relationship that I thought might have the potential for some permanence. Again, although I liked her parents and I think they liked me, it didn't work out. I did, however, give it some more effort.

Our last non-flying event was a brief, yet torturous, two-day training exercise in survival, evasion, resistance and escape (SERE) conducted at Ft. Stewart. We were introduced to survival techniques, including catching and preparing food, building shelter and avoiding capture. If captured, we were instructed in resistance techniques, what we could legally disclose to the enemy and what we could expect in the way of treatment and finally methods of escape. The final exercise began at dusk and required us to catch and prepare a meal, then make a movement over several miles of wooded terrain while avoiding capture. If captured (I was), we were subjected to mild harassment including being tied up and held in wooden cages for several hours, exposed to heavy smoke (from a nearby fire), and sprayed with water (temperatures were quite cool). Early in the morning, we were released and returned to base, exhausted but none the worse for wear. We never had any actual physical abuse; however, we were under no illusion as to what capture by the actual enemy would involve, certainly not the relatively tame treatment we had received during training.

Our last flight at Hunter was a massive formation with two flights of 16 aircraft each. We did a couple of flybys over Ft. Stewart and the main complex at Hunter. This event was followed by a formal dance the night before graduation.

My mother had flown to Savannah from Moberly for the graduation ceremony and would drive back to Missouri with me. While we were doing our last flight, she drove to Statesboro and picked up my girlfriend Diane and brought her back for the dance and ceremony. Mom and I dropped her off in Statesboro on our way back to Missouri. I graduated May 6, 1969.

Several of the Marines in my class were staying at Hunter for qualification in the AH-1 Cobra. I had orders to Marine Corps Air Station, Helicopter (MCAS [H]) Santa Ana (located in Tustin, California) for qualification in the CH-53 Sea Stallion; Hank was going to Tustin to fly the CH-46 Phrog.

While in Moberly on leave, I contracted with a local flight instructor to begin training for a private pilot's license in fixed-wing aircraft. For the last eight months, every time I flew I had been in a flight suit (looks like coveralls) and boots, so that's how I showed up for my first civilian flight lesson. My instructor was dressed rather casually in nice

9. Advanced Flight Training

shirt and slacks and soon set me straight as to what I needed to wear. After that, I was a lot more comfortable.

Civilian flight training in many ways is very similar to military flight training. We began by discussing some of the principles of flight, then walked around the aircraft conducting a preflight inspection to ensure the aircraft was ready to fly. After that, we strapped in (civilian aircraft had seat belts long before cars), started the aircraft and taxied to the end of the runway to prepare for takeoff. Taxiing a fixed-wing aircraft is much simpler than taxing a helicopter with skids for landing gear since the helicopter must hover to taxi, and the fixed-wing aircraft doesn't leave the ground until the takeoff sequence.

Flight school graduation party with my mother, Hunter Army Airfield, Savannah.

Takeoffs and landings are next, then stalls and other emergency procedures, and short and soft field landings. Much of your required training time is spent on cross-county flight. Since you are paying for the aircraft by the hour, this is where a large portion of the cost of training resides. Fortunately for my budget, I already had significant cross-county flight training and my civilian instructor had a contract to fly inspections on pipelines, so I accompanied him on those flights. When I left Moberly to head for California, I had a significant start on obtaining my private pilot's license.

10

Final Qualification, MCAS(H) Santa Ana

Tustin, California, 1969

I checked into Third Marine Aircraft Wing (3rdMAW) headquarters located at Marine Corps Air Station, El Toro, California, and was assigned to Marine Heavy Helicopter Training Squadron 301 (HMHT-301), MCAS (H), Santa Ana, the CH-53 training squadron for qualification in the CH-53 aircraft. After completing qualification, I would be sent to Vietnam. Hank was assigned to Marine Medium Helicopter Training Squadron 302 (HMMT-302) to learn to fly the CH-46.

Finally, on a Marine base I would no longer be drawing TAD money to cover the cost of living without a permanent assignment. However, there was no room available in the BOQ, so I was going to be paid a quarter's allowance to live in town. I don't know why Hank and I didn't choose to live together while in Southern California—after all, the squadrons were right next to each other—but we went our separate ways.

I rented a one-bedroom apartment in a nice area sort of between Tustin and Santa Ana, about a ten-minute drive to the airfield. The apartment complex was new construction, and I was the first occupant of my apartment. Several Marines who had been classmates during army flight training were either in this complex or nearby, including one who was keeping a small python as a pet. I think the python was really the idea of his girlfriend who, at any parties, was known to harbor the reptile inside her clothing. This was my first time without my best friend Hank in the last nine months. I learned later that Hank got out of the Marine Corps after Vietnam and became an FBI agent. He died not long after retiring from the FBI.

Training in the CH-53 would progress through several stages including familiarization (FAM), instrument (INST), formation

10. Final Qualification, MCAS(H) Santa Ana

(FORM), confined-area landings (CAL) and external operations (EXT) with each training flight lasting 90 minutes. I think there were about ten flights in the FAM stage, six or eight INST hops and a number of FORM, CAL and EXT flights for a total of about 50 flight hours of training. For those of us who came through the army pipeline, there would also be an instrument check flight before we could get our gold wings. (We were awarded silver U.S. Army wings when we completed training at Hunter, but a naval aviator is awarded gold wings.) Somehow, this training did not include carrier qualification training, probably because most of the aviators coming through this phase had done that while training with the navy at Pensacola.

Flying the '53 was fairly easy; learning the complex systems, not so much. My greatest difficulty was learning to get everything out of the aircraft there was to get. I tended to fly at a fairly shallow attitude which resulted in a slower-than-normal speed, mostly from my comfort with the Huey. Once I learned the aircraft, it became easier. FAM and INST training went well, and at the end of the INST phase I was scheduled for instrument ground school and then an instrument check flight. In instrument ground school, we learned about weather minimums, flight regulations and how to file an instrument flight plan.

As luck would have it, the weather on the day I was supposed to fly the check was crappy: low ceilings and visibility, just all-around bad weather, forecast to improve only marginally over the next couple of hours—a really unusual situation for Southern California. I was scheduled to fly with a senior major who held a "special instrument rating." A special card holder is allowed to take off in below minimum conditions if there was a forecast improvement. When I briefed the major about the weather, I told him that we were lucky; we could go because he had a special card, while everybody else would have to cancel. He then gave me some of the best advice I've ever had; he said, "The only thing I've learned in all the years it took to get a special instrument rating is that if it takes a special rating to go, then don't!" I have tried to keep that advice close ever since, and it might be part of what has allowed me to be successful in the air. My instrument check flight was rescheduled for later and I completed it successfully.

Nightlife in Southern California in the summer of 1969 was fast, loud and liquid. Every Friday after Happy Hour, I went to a different club and trolled for a date, unfortunately without much success. I don't think the hippies there really liked people in uniform. I had a good time anyway. One of the residents of my apartment complex was a recording studio musician and assisted with (played the electronic piano) the recording of "Light My Fire" by the Doors.

After completion of all the FAM and INST stage flights and a successful instrument check, each of the army-trained pilots was scheduled to be "winged" (awarded our gold wings) by the commanding general of the 3rdMAW in separate ceremonies. We were allowed to bring a "significant other" with us to the ceremony. I was not seeing anyone at the time, and Sally, the wife of a friend of mine, asked if she could go with me. Her husband, Al, was scheduled to get his wings the next week and she wanted to see what it entailed.

Sally went with me for the ceremony and helped pin the shiny new wings on my uniform shirt. I don't think to this day that the general realized that Sally wasn't my wife, just a friend.

After the "winging" ceremony, I went to Orange County Airport and contracted to complete my fixed-wing training, and after several flights there, I was scheduled for a check ride. I completed it successfully, and after the flight I received my private license with ratings in fixed and rotary wing, with rotary wing instrument qualification.

In July of that summer, I visited my mother's cousins in Northridge, located just north of Los Angeles and watched the first man walk on the moon!

I got a bit of a scare that summer. Someone broke into my car (didn't take it on a joy ride this time) and attempted to get into my locked glove compartment. Fortunately, they were not successful; that was where my revolver was stored. I ended up with a lecture from the Tustin police officer who investigated the break-in about the safe storage of weapons. If that had happened today, they would have confiscated my unregistered weapon. Unfortunately, this time my 8-tracks were gone!

Just after getting my gold wings, now designated as a naval aviator.

10. Final Qualification, MCAS(H) Santa Ana

I completed advanced flight training with HMHT-301 on September 18 and prepared to deploy to Vietnam. I packed my personal belongings and arranged to have them shipped back to my hometown, Moberly, Missouri. I sold my Camaro (I still regret that) and flew home via St. Louis. Mom and Dad picked me up there.

11

Moberly, Missouri
Fall 1969

While on leave before departing for Vietnam, I spent some time reconnecting with friends and taking care of some personal business, like making out a will. I had no thoughts of not making it back in one piece, but a will seemed like a wise move and good preparation.

Since I had my private fixed-wing certificate, I made arrangements to borrow one of the aircraft from the company where my mother worked and fly back to Statesboro, Georgia, to see Diane, my flight school girlfriend. Bad weather en route caused me to cancel that plan, and I never saw her again. Another potential permanent relationship dashed on the rocks of fate. Better things were coming; I just didn't know it yet.

With my visit to Georgia canceled, I decided to visit my brother at Culver-Stockton College in Canton, Missouri. The weekend I visited, the campus was mostly empty except for a few friends of his. We got together with them for a few drinks. While there, I met one of his friends and his wife. They joined us for an evening out. Later that night after many (too many) drinks, we crashed at my brother's fraternity house. After sleeping in for a while, I headed back to Moberly with a significant headache.

With nothing else on my calendar, I finally quit putting it off and called for an appointment with an attorney who was a family friend and a partner in the firm of Hunter, Chamier and Lee to make out my will. One of the partners was the father of one of my high school classmates and another was a friend from church. So I thought this was keeping it in the family.

When I arrived for my appointment, I was greeted by a gorgeous young lady with long, wavy red hair and a short, short miniskirt. I have always been able to talk to strangers, so we had a pretty good conversation before I went in to see the attorney. When I went back to pick up my will, I talked to her at length again and asked her out (did I mention she had a short miniskirt and great legs?). In the long run, this encounter worked out pretty well, although we only had one or two dates before my deployment.

My deployment date crept up on me quickly and I was unable to schedule any additional dates before heading to Vietnam. My personal belongings, flight gear and uniforms that were shipped from California had not arrived, so I had to scramble a bit to try and locate my rather essential gear. As it turned out, my stuff was being shipped by a trucking company that was owned by the brother of the man who owned the company where my mother worked. A couple of phone calls by him and my stuff showed up in time for my deployment. It helps to have friends, especially friends who own trucking companies.

Just before leaving Moberly, I visited Connor's Sporting Goods, a local landmark specializing in outdoor sporting goods. While there, I purchased a ten-inch Buck knife and sheath that I carried on every flight in Vietnam. My thoughts were that with that knife I could cut my way out of a crashed aircraft with little difficulty. I still have that knife and occasionally get it out to show it off.

12

En Route to Vietnam
Fall 1969

After flying from St. Louis to Los Angeles, my real journey to Vietnam began at March AFB, just outside of Los Angeles. The aircraft was an older model Boeing 707 operated by Tiger Airlines. Our intended routing would take us from Los Angeles through an air force base in Alaska, then on to Okinawa. Unfortunately, the aircraft developed a mechanical problem after leaving Alaska and diverted to Honolulu, Hawaii. We spent the next five hours sitting in the Honolulu Airport bar waiting on repairs. For many years afterward, my familiarity with Hawaii consisted of five hours in the airport bar. The libations we were able to obtain made the remainder of the trip quite pleasant (since I slept through most of it). Finally, underway, we arrived in Okinawa some 20 hours after leaving California.

At this point, I thought we were going to refuel and continue to Vietnam. Little did I know! The actual plan had us off-loading and spending from three to seven days in Okinawa, beginning our acclimatization process and providing some free labor for a few essential (to somebody) tasks. I was initially assigned to a warehouse supervising a working party of young Marines that was counting and folding blankets.

I managed to get off the base and out on the town a few times. At one point, I called my mom and reported on my progress (toward Vietnam). Mom told me about a high school classmate who had married an air force officer who was assigned to Kadena AFB, also located on Okinawa. I was able to call my classmate and went to Kadena and had dinner with her and her husband. Her husband's father was a television repairman and had been to our house many times to repair the older model television we owned.

The only eventful things happening in Okinawa at the time involved lots of alcohol and some pretty good food. While in town, I visited several local eateries and sampled some significantly fine cuisine. Perhaps my favorite was Kobe beef with bean sprouts prepared at the table! Okinawa was also my introduction to massage therapy. A steam bath followed by a full-body massage was a great finish to a hard night of drinking.

Eventually, I was assigned a flight on to Vietnam. It was also a Tiger Airlines 707. It didn't have any mechanical problems, and we arrived safely at Da Nang AFB, Da Nang, South Vietnam, on October 21, 1969, where we immediately went by "cattle car" to the in-processing center, located just west of Da Nang AFB at a place called Freedom Hill. Marines leaving Vietnam for rest and relaxation (R&R) or for return to the States were also processed through the facility at Freedom Hill.

13

South Vietnam
October 21, 1969–September 30, 1970

October in Vietnam was hot; in fact, I don't remember any month that wasn't hot. I guess some months were not as hot as others, some hotter.

After clearing the processing center, aviation personnel reported to their assigned units and began a short period of acclimatization and orientation. I reported to MAG-16 as a qualified, yet inexperienced, H2P (helicopter second pilot or copilot) in the mighty CH-53A. The S-1 (Admin) at group headquarters said, "Crap, we've got more '53 pilots than we know what to do with, and we are about to send one squadron back to the States. Have you flown anything else?" I replied that I had gone through the army flight training program and the last third of the training was in H-1s. He was happy with that and assigned me to HML-167 to fly the UH-1E. Although I had flown the H-1 model aircraft in flight school, I had not flown the "E" series aircraft. As it turned out, the "E" was very similar to the "C" model I had flown; the only real difference was the "E" had a rotor brake installed for shipboard operations (one friend said it was so we could debrief and get to the club faster).

The check-in process to MAG-16 took several days to complete. With limited bus service and an absence of any other vehicular transportation available, I had to walk everywhere and generally wait at each location while the process was handled, usually just finding someone to sign the check-in sheet. Rarely was there any other significant reason for "checking in." At least at the supply building, we were issued wet-weather gear. There were several of us checking in at the same time, and for the first few days we were billeted together in temporary housing consisting of a 16- by 32-foot wooden structure with half-height wooden walls called a Southeast Asian hut (SEA hut). The top half of the walls was screen wire with closable shutters. For sleeping, we had cots

13. South Vietnam

and a blanket. No AC and no fans. I was really looking forward to getting to better accommodations, maybe when I actually got to HML-167. Did I mention it was hot out?

The "checkmates" of HML-167 began life in April 1968 with 10 pilots and 11 aircraft. That month, they flew 596 hours, leading to a total of 31,615 hours as of February 1970. HML-167 started life as a "company grade" squadron, with a major as commanding officer. The squadron was formed with UH-1Es and pilots from VMO-2, which was transitioning to the OV-10, Bronco. Initially, some UH-34 pilots began transitioning to the 1E as HMM-361 began transitioning to the CH-53A, while VMO-2 continued to loan pilots as needed. By October 1968, HML-167 was flying independently from VMO; by the end of the year, the 45-strong of 167 was averaging 1,500 hours a month. The maintenance department was providing outstanding support with 81 percent availability. Many of these hours were flown in support of Operation Meade River; the squadron completed its first 10,000 hours in December 1968, less than nine months after activation.

In 1969, more hours were flown in support of Operations Taylor Common, Dewey Canyon, Linn River and Pipestone Canyon. During the first half of 1969, the slicks carried notable VIPs such as Defense Secretary Laird, Ambassador and Mrs. Bunker, Ambassador MacKelhose of New Zealand, Chairman of the Joint Chiefs General Wheeler, General Abrams, Commanding General MACV and Senator Stevens of Alaska.

Typical Southeast Asia (SEA) hut.

The first squadron office, April 1968, HML-167.

The summer and fall of 1969 brought an influx of lieutenants from continental United States and in December, HML-167 received more UH-1Es and pilots from HML-367 as they moved from Phu Bai and transitioned to the AH-1G Cobras. HML-167 was not only the only squadron to be formed in a combat zone, but it was also then the largest squadron in the Marine Corps. In its first 12 months of existence, it had four different commanding officers and six different XOs.

Once I got to HML-167, there was more "checking in" to do. Generally, the first seven days in country were used to adjust to the heat and humidity and the change in time zones. We were not allowed to fly until this period was over, circadian rhythms and all that stuff. During daylight hours (normal working hours for support facilities), I accomplished the mundane process of checking in. At night, I spent significant time in the paraloft (the shop where flight equipment, including helmets, flight suits, survival equipment and in-jet squadrons' parachutes were maintained) working on my flight helmet. HML-167 had "nose art" on each of their aircraft consisting of a red-and-black "checkerboard" and another checkerboard painted horizontally across the vertical tail of the aircraft. Many of the pilots had replicated the design on their helmet visor cover and I intended to do the same.

Visor covers on our helmets are not quite rectangular and are curved in two dimensions with the top border being slightly shorter than the bottom. To paint the visor cover, it had to be removed from the

13. South Vietnam

Checkerboard nose art.

helmet. Thus I enlisted the supervisory help of the paraloft workers. The first night after disassembling the helmet, I applied a base coat of gloss black. The next night, I applied half-inch masking tape in a crisscross pattern. Getting it precisely measured and marked perfectly was a difficult task because of the curves and non-standard dimensions, but once that was accomplished, I applied a coat of gloss red. The third night (after sufficient drying), I removed the tape and, with the close supervision of paraloft personnel, reassembled my helmet. I was now ready to fly (at least I looked the part).

Another project that occupied my time was map preparation. Maps were maintained in S-2 (the intelligence office). We were issued a small, red Naugahyde (there was an abundance of red Naugahyde available) bag that contained 24 maps in the scale of 1 to 50,000 and numbered 1 to 24. At the speed we flew, we would quickly cross one of those maps and need another. To remedy that, we were also issued a 1 to 250,000 map that covered almost all of our TAOR (tactical area of responsibility). On this map, we would mark the location of the TACAN sites and draw radials every five degrees out from them. Then we would mark the radials for distance from the TACAN site. Many times, we would get a location of a unit based on the radial and distance measuring equipment from the TACAN. We also drew in the area represented by each of our 1 to 50,000 maps and numbered the rectangular drawings to correspond with the maps in the packet. Once that was complete, we would work with the intelligence people to laminate the map, then fold it accordion style to fit in the map pocket of our flight suits.

During the check-in process, I was assigned billeting in the squadron area, which was in Quonset huts similar to those open bay huts we had in boot camp. The difference was each hut was divided by internal walls into four quadrants. Each quadrant had some furnishings to add a little comfort to our lives. We each had a bed (a metal rack with a thin mattress, one grade up from a cot) and a small locker to store personal items. Now I had someplace to leave my "things" where they wouldn't be stolen. Three officers lived in each section, one of my hooch mates was Lt Rick Jenkins, Comprise 21, the other was Larry T (I have not been able to get in touch with Larry to use his name). Each section had an air conditioner, and at some point during our tour, each of us bought a mini fridge at the PX to keep drinks and snacks. Now I had two new friends, with more to come. "Hooch" maids, Vietnamese women who had been cleared to work on the base, worked in the housing area, cleaning the huts and doing laundry for the inhabitants. Each officer paid their "hooch maid" weekly, usually about $5. During our tour, our hooch maid's husband died of tuberculosis, so we had to be tested. Rick had a slight reaction, but it was not significant; Larry and I had no reaction.

Officer's hooches, officer's row, Marble Mountain Air Facility, RVN.

13. South Vietnam

I had no idea then how good we had it. Electricity was on at all times. We had a shower complex within 30 or 40 yards with hot running water and a place to shave and perform a daily "constitutional." The mess, adjacent to the officers' club, had hot meals three times daily with fresh fruits and vegetables. In his memoir, *Marble Mountain*, Bud Willis described the amenities at Marble Mountain as rather austere. Showers from a 55-gallon barrel hung in the sun for heating, cold water shaves and meals from canned products were what he had for creature comforts for most of his 13-month tour. When he first arrived, there were insufficient racks (beds), so as people were deployed to different areas, beds were shared.*

Me sitting outside my hooch.

The squadron Quonset huts assigned to HML-167 were located on the east side of the airfield, just north of the northern end of the runway. The officers' club and adjacent officers' mess was about 300 yards south of our huts. There were a number of SEA huts west and south of the officers' club. The runway orientation was north/south and the length of the runway about 5,000 feet. Our squadron hangar and aircraft parking area were also on the east side of the runway about halfway down the runway from the O club.

Next to my Quonset was a massive bunker dug into the ground about two or three feet and built out of a combination of sandbags, reinforced with Marston matting (normally used to construct a temporary airstrip). The entrance was next to the door of our hut. The top of the

---

* Willis, Bud, *Marble Mountain: A Vietnam Memoir*, AuthorHouse Publishing, 64–68.

bunker was layered with additional Marston matting, which made for an ideal suntanning facility.

Not long before my arrival in Vietnam, a new pilot for Flying Tigers Airlines landed his Boeing 707 at Marble Mountain instead of Da Nang. He was flying a visual flight rules approach and mistakenly lined up on our runway, which was significantly shorter than Da Nang's. All his passengers had to bus to Da Nang, the aircraft stripped of everything that could be removed and defueled to the minimum required to fly the two miles to Da Nang. A company check pilot had to be flown in to fly the aircraft from Marble Mountain to Da Nang. I'm not sure what happened to the pilot who left his plane on the end of our runway.

Most other pilots in HML-167 had gone through a training syllabus at Camp Pendleton, California, or at Marine Air Facility, New River, Jacksonville, North Carolina, to get rated as a pilot qualified in model (PQM) in the UH-1E, which is the initial qualification level for that type/model aircraft. In the CH-53 and the CH-46, you were initially qualified as an H2P while gaining experience. Eventually, you would qualify as a helicopter aircraft commander (HAC) after accumulating sufficient flight hours and experience in the aircraft and completing a Naval Air Training and Operating Procedures Standardization (NATOPS) flight check ride. I now had to do some semblance of the same syllabus plus local indoctrination before being turned loose on the enemy.

At the time, we had one lieutenant colonel, five majors (two of who were assigned permanent VIP duty with 1st MAW and III MAF) and three captains. The remainder of the pilots assigned to HML-167 were first lieutenants—about 25 or 30 of them. Rumor had it (and I never questioned the rumor) that the two majors assigned to permanent VIP duty had committed some faux pas, and rather than be trusted to support the troops in the field, they were assigned to missions where they couldn't get in trouble.

To get orientated in country, you fly a wide variety of missions as a copilot learning the terrain and routing to get out of and into Marble Mountain and Da Nang AFB. But before I could start flying, I had paperwork to do. First up was an open-book NATOPS exam. This was a paper exam of about 100 questions specific to the aircraft in which I would be qualifying. It had to be completed before my first flight. There also was a 20- or 30-question paper regarding airfield procedures. Later, there would be a shorter closed-book exam administered prior to getting a NATOPS check flight. (Final approval for being designated a PQM.) My qualification flights would be combined with my orientation flights, so I had some double learning to do. Fortunately, the UH-1E doesn't fly much different than the UH-1C or UH-1D models I had

13. South Vietnam

become familiar with during my army flight training. I did have to learn a different engine, although most of the systems were the same. Start sequence and checklist were the same. I had to study and be prepared to address systems failures and emergency procedures. I flew three or four times a week under close supervision while practicing Fam, INST, CALS and autorotations.

In the army training command, we shot autorotations to a full landing; in the Marine Corps, we terminated the autorotation with a "power recovery" never making it all the way to the ground. Learning to do a full auto really paid dividends for me years later. I was also introduced to gunship procedures and shooting. And finally, a NATOPS check ride so then I could start contributing.

HML-167 flight line with aircraft in the revetments. Our hangar is to the left.

14

First Flight

October 27, 1969, not quite a full week, but I am scheduled for my first flight. It is a 5:00 a.m. brief for a 7:00 a.m. launch on Mission 1 (chase aircraft support for the commanding general, III MAF). We actually launch at 0655 and return to Marble Mountain at 1645 (4:45 p.m.). The flight is with one of the majors assigned to VIP duty and lasts two hours. (Lots of sitting and waiting time.) I am introduced to basic procedures for getting into and out of Marble Mountain, Da Nang AFB, and several of the landing zones that are associated with various headquarters. As it turns out, this is the only flight during my year in Vietnam that the after-action report shows that I got one hour of familiarization training. My next three flights were also with majors, two from the group headquarters and one more flight with the original VIP pilot. My fifth flight of the month was with a lieutenant, and it covered four and a half hours over multiple tasks through several landing zones. On November 1, I had another flight with a lieutenant for 6.9 hours, which covered a multitude of missions and locations.

Finally, on my first gunship mission, led by our XO, I am flying in the second aircraft with a lieutenant. The XO briefed procedures for covering the Phrogs. After getting a zone brief from the ground unit, we would circle the area staying at altitude and clear of the transport aircraft. We would only react to the transports taking fire from some identifiable area. The mission is a resupply for the Fifth Marines working out of An Hoa airfield and will take a couple of hours. These artificial restrictions were meant to keep us safe while still providing sufficient protection for the transport aircraft. (Remember in the preface I talked about field grade officers being too cautious and how we [company grade officers, particularly the lieutenants] bristled about restrictions.) I learned some 55 years later where these restrictions came from. Rick Jenkins, my roommate, said that our XO proposed and enforced several "standards" that we were to follow.

14. First Flight

LZ 11, the landing pad for wing headquarters.

Every morning, he would inspect the gunships to ensure his artificial limit of 4,000 rounds of 7.62-mm ammunition was all that was stored on the aircraft. Jenks said he had a one-day grounding because his aircraft had more ammo than what was allowed. I can possibly understand the XO's rationale for the limit since our aircraft were weight limited; however, by managing our fuel load, we could easily handle more ammunition. With the distances between most of our missions being fairly close and fuel readily available, a limited fuel load did not adversely affect our support of the ground troops or protection for the transport folks. Jenks said he was not an accuracy guy, more of a volume guy, and limiting the number of rounds we carried cramped his style. (With our aiming system, I can easily understand that.) Once we were airborne, the lieutenant I was flying with said that everything the XO had briefed was BS, and if we got into a "shoot 'em up," he would show me how it was really done. The "shoot 'em up" didn't happen that day, and we completed our mission without incident.

I was taught during my gunship orientation flights with field grade officers that when escorting aircraft on various missions, we should orbit at or above 1,000 feet and watch for enemy action, then react to the threat. Most ordnance that was expended by field grade officers was at altitude, was not delivered accurately and they did not pursue the enemy. In discussions with some transport pilots, I found that they did not trust our field grade officers to support them properly, which led to the ditty frequently heard in drunk fests in the O club: "Comprise, Comprise," please come down out of the sky, we don't want to die. (Comprise was our squadron call sign and sometimes over frequent alcoholic libations was modified to "Compromise.")

Our rocket aiming system was very inaccurate, and to provide accurate fire support, we really needed to get lower. Initially, our rockets were the F-102 model, which were designed to be used on jet aircraft and lacked some performance when fired from a slower helicopter, particularly with the deployment of their fins at low airspeeds. Later, we got the model 104, which performed much better (all four fins deployed each time one was fired). Company grade tactics generally had the lead gunship rolling in with the lead Phrog in his "death spiral,"* then passing him as he slowed for his final approach. The second gunship would then roll in as the lead pulled off (usually to the right). Pullout would be around 200 feet, and the door guns would be used to cover our pull. The purpose of this maneuver was to intimidate as well as locate the enemy. Seeing a gunship rolling in on their position was a clear signal for the enemy to keep their heads down and not attempt anything foolish, like shooting at the Phrog; additionally, the "two-bladed slap" of our rotor heads as we pulled out of a gun run was intimidating all by itself.

The "death spiral" was a maneuver where the aircraft arrived over the zone at 1,000 feet, lowered the collective, rolled to maximum angle of bank and pointed the nose at the ground. In one rapid 360 degree turn, the aircraft would lose all its altitude and arrive over the zone for a no or minimum hover landing.

Later in my tour, we were introduced to the fléchette warhead for our rockets. This ordnance was designed to be used against troops in the open. Each warhead contained hundreds of tiny steel "arrows" that would deploy after the warhead had armed and exploded. The "arrows" were about an inch and a half long, about an eighth of an inch in diameter and had four permanent fins to provide stable flight. The only problem was the rocket had to be fired at a sufficient distance so that the warhead would arm. One of our majors fired a pair of fléchette rockets too close to the ground, the rockets did not arm, just imbedded themselves in the sandy soil they had impacted.

---

* Walker, Harold G., *The Grotto*, Book Two, Dragonfly Publishing, 260.

14. First Flight   67

Unfortunately, the major just provided the enemy with two very powerful sets of booby trap material.

When I was released to fly on my own, I, like all those proceeding me, was assigned some of the simpler missions, such as picking up VIPs at Da Nang AFB and dropping them someplace else.

Trips to LZ 400 (division headquarters) and LZ 11 (wing headquarters) were plentiful. Mixed in were trips to the Republic of Korea (ROK) headquarters, called Land of the Blue Dragon, just south of Marble Mountain and adjacent to the Arizona Territory as well as Hill 55, LZ Baldy, An Hoa airfield and others.

Meals for officers were served in a mess (dining area) located in an annex to the officers' club near the main billeting area, where we could eat three meals a day (if we ever had time, we were lucky to squeeze in one meal a day, usually breakfast before the first brief). When we couldn't eat, we had C rations available. I really don't remember much about it; meals were kind of plain, nothing to write home about except for Sunday nights. The club broke out the grills and served steak with all the fixings every Sunday. Even if we couldn't get to church (services were available if we weren't flying), we got to steak night.

Everyone who has been a Marine knows that if you stand in an airport or an officers' club long enough, someone you previously served

North end of MMAF. The officers' club is in the center and officers' hooches are to the right.

with will eventually walk up and say hello (even with us relatively new guys)! One day, I remember standing in line waiting my turn to get some chow and thinking the second lieutenant behind me really looked familiar and then it hit me. He was formerly one of my DIs from boot camp, a staff sergeant then, now a second lieutenant. He had an aviation maintenance background and had gotten a commission as a limited-duty officer and was sent to Vietnam as an aviation maintenance officer. It was good to visit with him, but our paths did not cross again.

Everybody also gets a nickname. You don't get to choose your nickname; you earn it, or it is given to you by those around you, friends and others. As HML-367 received Cobras (AH-1Gs), they parted with their UH-1Es (they were transferred to us along with some of their lieutenants). We expanded, growing to over 50 lieutenants and eventually (early 1970) a few more captains and a major or two. Total pilot strength was over 60 officers.

Obviously, we couldn't go by the names our parents had assigned us; there had to be some variant that made sense to those around us. Some of these new name assignments came from the times we lived in, our appearance or our background. Some had no rhyme or reason, but they all stuck. The nicknames were unique, and you didn't get to pick your own; in some cases, these names became your call sign. My friends included a lanky, slow-talking man named George who was from south Missouri; he became "Lonesome George" from George Gobel. Another was Lt Milt Matthews, Comprise 32, himself an amateur comedian, so he was "Uncle Milty" from Milton Berle, a famous comedian and variety show performer from the '50s and early '60s. One of my roommates, Lt Rick Jenkins, Comprise 21, became "Jenks," a variation of his last name. Lt Tom Broderick, who became one of my best friends after Vietnam, was known as Two-Two, from the two crashes he was involved in. He was shot down on his first Fam hop in country, then shot down again a few months later. He was the only survivor from the second crash. One of our majors was "The Owl," also a variation of his last name. One captain whose first name was Marv became "Marvelous Marv" from Marvelous Marv Thornberry. Lt Mike Smith, Comprise 15, had the initials M.A. He was using his initials to distinguish himself from another Smith, Lt J.R. (Rusty) Smith, Comprise 25. Mike became MA1, from the military designation of the wet compass in the aircraft. And of course Lt Elmer Davis, Comprise 47, was "Fudd" from the Bugs Bunny comedy. Another captain whose last name was "Hammer" became "Mike" from the TV detective show.

There were three "Joes" in the squadron. Lt Joel Hall, Comprise 35, who I thought was of Indian descent, became "Injun Joe." He recently

14. First Flight

A Comprise Huey in the fuel pits.

told me he was not Indian; he thought his nickname came from his use of "firewater" (political correctness had not struck yet, and we wouldn't have cared). I, Comprise 11, was the smallest of the three "Joes," so I was "Little Joe" or sometimes "Lil Joe." One of the few non-aviator officers in our unit was our aviation supply officer, a tall, muscular, black officer who became "Just Plain Joe." Our XO, a major who had previously signed us to our army aviation contracts, was "Speedy." But since no one could call him that to his face, we named the squadron dog "Speedy."

Soon after arriving "in country," everybody gets sent to Cubi Point Naval Air Station in the Philippines for four days of jungle environmental survival training (JEST). During the last few weeks at Hunter Army Airfield, we had an abbreviated SERE course over the course of a couple of days. This was supposed to be a more intensive, focused training session over three days with specific emphasis on surviving in the jungle environment. After my first three flights in November, it was my turn.

The actual training involved a half day in the classroom and a half day in the jungle (about 200 yards in from the classroom) identifying edible plants, learning to construct a shelter and build a fire. There were all things I had done in the Boy Scouts, although the edible plants were somewhat different. The rest of the three or four days there was spent in the bars of Olongapo, throwing coins in "Sh*t" River (a small river that divided the city of Olongapo from the base and was the repository of the open city sewers) for the young boys in their dugout canoes to dive for and recover (none of which I had done in the Boy Scouts) and checking out the wares in the Navy Exchange.

I purchased a high-quality Minolta SLR 35 mm camera, which I carried on every mission I flew over the next year. To deter high-dollar purchases that would end up on the black market (in town), the registration and verification process was somewhat extensive, but I did manage to navigate those waters and came home with the camera. I did not always have time to take pictures, but I had the camera. You will see a few of those pictures throughout this book.

Cubi Point is also a port, so the place was packed with sailors from ships making a port of call while refreshing their stores. Sailors on liberty kept the bars hopping and the girls even busier.

The bars of Olongapo had several commonalities: cheap liquor, loud music played by Filipino bands closely imitating U.S. and English bands, and lots of scantily clad women. How good they looked under the soft bar lights and with the effects of alcohol was significantly different than their looks early in the morning. Every one of these women was looking for a husband to take her back to the United States. The most commonly heard phrase in any bar was "I love you, GI. No sh*t!" I don't need to describe what occurred each night there as the sailors sought companionship and the girls sought husbands.

The gates to Cubi Point closed at midnight. At that time, you were either in or out. If out, it was time to seek shelter (with companionship). You did not want to be on the streets after midnight; the Olongapo police were nasty and did not appreciate having to deal with drunk Marines and sailors. I was able to sober up enough to catch the flight back to Vietnam at the end of my three days.

We went through three commanding officers while I was assigned to HML-167, the first LtCol had his change of command on November 8, just 19 days after I arrived. The second LtCol was nicknamed "Black Jack," possibly a reference to his drinking habits. I rarely saw him in the club, so he must have been a "closet drinker." That change of command was April 9, 1970, and the final commanding officer was a former Blue Angels pilot. I didn't have much experience with the first commanding officer, the second was a major disappointment and, unfortunately, a major impediment to anyone seeking a career in the Marine Corps, especially if you were not on his list of favorites. The last was really a good guy, a good pilot and a positive influence on all of us.

Several generals came out of this squadron including Major

14. First Flight

General (MGen) Ross Plasterer, and General Mike Williams. From the '46 squadron on the other side of the runway from us was Lieutenant General (LtGen) Fred McCorkle and LtGen Mike DeLong.

After returning from Cubi Point, flying resumed in earnest. I celebrated the Marine Corps Birthday flying with the XO, while we carried the chief of staff, III MAF, Brigadier General (BGen) Dooley to several locations. Then on November 11 while flying the afternoon gunship escort for the medevac Phrogs, I received my first enemy fire. We returned the favor with 38 rockets and 2,500 rounds of machine gun fire, while evacuating seven wounded Marines over three and a half hours. The next day, it's a 5.5-hour armed escort for resupplying the Fifth Marines out of An Hoa, and the enemy shot at us again. Since I was flying with a major and we couldn't positively identify where the fire came from, we did not return fire. I flew everyday for the rest of the month, mostly with lieutenants in VIP hops. Then on the 24th, a four-hour gunship escort for medevac for six wounded Marines. That wrapped up November, completing a 64.9-hour month.

I should mention that I was a terrible letter writer; I would much prefer to pick up the phone and call. Unfortunately, we had no phones here and I was totally unaware of the MARS station where you could make calls home via ham radio operators. Writing was a painful ordeal for me. The lack of writing contributed significantly to me joining the Marine Corps, and it finally led to me getting called to the squadron commanding officer's office about three months into my tour. I had failed to keep in contact with my parents after I left Okinawa, and Mom had contacted the Red Cross for a "wellness" check. After that, I made an effort to write at least once every week or two. Sometimes I was actually successful. Later, I learned that you could use the high-frequency radio in the aircraft to contact an air force base in St. Louis and they would connect you via landline to your loved ones.

Most evenings were spent in the O club, drinking copious amounts of alcohol and singing raucously to many familiar tunes. One of our favorites was the Animals' "We Gotta Get Outta This Place."

Another was the "Marble" song:

> Marble, oh Marble, a hell of a place,
> The organization's a f**king disgrace,
> With captains and majors and light colonels too,
> Thumbs up their asses, with nothing to do.
> They stand on the runway, they scream, and they shout,
> About all the things they know nothing about,
> For all they accomplish, they might as well be
> Shoveling shit in the South China Sea.

> Ring a ding, a ding-ding, blow it out your ass,
> You'll wonder where the yellow went,
> when the H-bomb hits the Orient.
> Nuke 'em, Nuke 'em, Nuke 'em.
> Ho Chi Minh is dead.*

Also known as the Phu Bai song, just substitute Phu Bai, oh Phu Bai for Marble, oh Marble.

Part of orientation training was an introduction to the routes south from Marble Mountain to the Arizona Territory, Go Noi Island, LZ Baldy, Hill 55, FSB Ross, An Hoa Airfield, Hoi An, the Que Son mountains and others. There was a complex network that combined the names of states and cities for the routing, but when working escort for the transport aircraft (CH-46s and CH-53s), we had to cut corners since our overloaded aircraft cruised at a slightly slower airspeed than the faster transports. When getting clearance from HDC, we usually just called clear Marble, Red Line (Highway 1) south to the Blue Line (Thu Bon River), then west to … wherever. We often followed the "Big Sky, Little Bullet" theory.

Crew chiefs deserve their own book; their contribution to the war in Vietnam is immeasurable. Without them, we didn't fly. I have not mentioned many names of crew chiefs in these chapters, but each one was the guy that was always there. Most were fresh out of high school, young men serving their country to the best of their ability and growing up fast. They had no control of their fate; they depended on the skill and ability of their pilot, but they contributed to the successful completion of the mission every day and every time. Without them, it didn't get done. They were America's hope for the future. They are still out there every day performing their duties with every squadron in the Marine Corps, doing what they do best. Their performance is under-recognized.

Bud Willis in his memoir said after a particularly harrowing mission, "I wanted to buy the crew chief a drink, but he was not allowed in the Officer's Club. One of the biggest problems with the military is that the guys who really know what they are doing are enlisted people, and the young, green officers are not allowed to fraternize with them. Most of us college boys would be lost without the rugged common sense and stamina of the Marine enlisted men. Each one of them has been honed for a particular military occupational specialty. In addition, every one of them, regardless of their specialty, is a skilled rifleman."†

Two brothers, Tom and Jim Whiteside, were my high school

---

* Walker, Harold G., *The Grotto*, Book One, Dragonfly Publishing, 313–314.
† Willis, Bud, *Marble Mountain: A Vietnam Memoir*, AuthorHouse Publishing, 217.

classmates and served in Vietnam at the same time as I. Tom was a senior when I was a sophomore, and Jim was in my class. Both, in turn, were quarterbacks of our high school football team. Tom was a captain and the commander of an amtrac unit just south of Marble Mountain, and Jim served in a motor transport unit west of Da Nang. One day when I wasn't flying, I got some friends to drop me off to visit with Tom, but I never caught up with Jim while in country.

15

Qualifications and Designations

Phrogs (CH-46) and Hogs (CH-53), also known as "Shitters" because of things falling off them or being dropped by them, are transport aircraft designated as "multi-pilot aircraft." There is a qualification for a H2P, which is the copilot for that aircraft. The Huey is a single pilot aircraft (even though we operated all of the gunships and some of the slicks with two pilots). In the Huey, there is no designation for "copilot." For all of the helicopters in Vietnam, the pilots underwent a basic qualification syllabus in the States before arriving in Vietnam. That resulted in pilots arriving as PQM for the Huey pilots and either HAC or H2P for the transport aircraft. Obviously, I was a special case as was Injun Joe Hall since we were transitioned from the CH-53 to the Huey in country. This turned out to be true for a few other pilots as well when one of the '53 squadrons was pulled out of country and their pilots were left behind.

In the transport aircraft, being eligible for advancement to HAC was based on several factors, including flight time in the aircraft, experience, total flight time and a recommendation from other pilots he has flown with. Advancement required the pilot to complete an additional closed-book examination (usually more rigorous than that completed for the H2P designation) and a check flight conducted with a pilot designated as qualified to conduct such a flight examination by the squadron commander. A 7.2-hour HAC check in the CH-46 is described by Harold Walker.*

Once a pilot is designated as PQM or HAC, they become eligible to receive advanced designations. Among those designations are section leader (leads a flight of two aircraft), division leader (leads a flight of two sections), flight leader (leads multiple divisions) or mission commander

---

* Walker, Harold G., *The Grotto*, Book Two, Dragonfly Publishing, 221–225.

15. Qualifications and Designations

(leads multiple flights of diverse aircraft tasked to accomplish a specific large-scale mission). A mission commander would usually fly in a "command and control" aircraft equipped with a set of special radios where he would direct the accomplishment of the mission. Rarely, if ever, would he be flying the aircraft. These designations are based on experience in the aircraft and are at the discretion of the squadron commanding officer based on recommendations of his staff.

The mission commander role is exemplified in Chapter 50, "Overloaded Medevac," with BGen Miller acting as mission commander for a regimental-level insert into bad-guy country also in Chapter 24, "Eagle Claw."

16

Experiments with Weapons

Vietnam was a proving ground for what kinds of weapons we could hang on a helicopter. The Cobras were carrying a 19-shot rocket pod, so why couldn't the Hueys also take advantage of the additional ordnance? The mounting points were the same for the 7-shot pod as for the 19-shot pod; the electrical connection to fire the rockets was the same. So why not?

Actually, the answer was pretty simple: weight! Twelve extra rockets on each side of the aircraft added plenty of firepower (and weight). The extra weight meant that we had to reduce the fuel load even further. Another option was to not load all 19 tubes. That would have been OK; we would have sufficient fuel to get anywhere in the TAOR and to support the troops on the ground or protect the transports. Finding the optimal number would not be hard. That left only one problem: if all the tubes were not loaded with a rocket, then the rockets had to be loaded in a certain order. The electrical firing system was sequenced to certain tubes. If the tubes were out of order, we could be attempting to fire a rocket out of a tube that did not contain a rocket. If we were in a gun run when that happened, we might not be able to support the transports or troops to the best of our ability. This would put an additional burden on our crew chiefs and gunners, who would be required to perform this task perfectly while under extreme pressure. As much as they were already doing, the additional pressure was not reasonable.

Additionally, the number of available 19-shot pods was limited, so it made sense that they should all be available to the Cobras, who could fully utilize them. So, after a limited trial run, this idea was dropped.

Another idea with some promise was helicopter trap weapon, known as "Daisy Cutters." These were small bombs that sent shrapnel

16. Experiments with Weapons

Comprise Huey with 19-shot rocket pods.

out about 30 meters, four to six inches off the ground. They were fairly effective in clearing a landing zone for the transport aircraft.

We could mount four of these on a bomb rack that had the same mounting fixtures as our seven-shot pods. The bomb racks were available since they were the same as ones used on the A-4. The electrical sequence for dropping them utilized the same wiring as our rocket pod, so it was a very simple conversion.

The problem with this experiment was tactics and employment. If we loaded the Daisy Cutters, then one of our gunships was short of 14 rockets, and we didn't have enough spare aircraft to send out a third gun loaded with Daisy

Lt Tom Broderick beside a Huey loaded with helicopter trap weapon.

Cutters. Additionally, if we were trying to clear a zone when troops were on the ground, how far away should they be? We certainly didn't want to create more injuries. Not sure how we ever solved this; probably, the best solution would be to utilize them for inserts with recon only.

17

Intramural and Social Activities

When we weren't flying, we were assigned collateral duties. In a normal Marine Corps squadron, the structure goes like this. At the top is a lieutenant colonel, whose primary billet is listed as the commanding officer. Then there are normally five majors whose billets in order of seniority are the XO, the operations officer (Ops O or S3), the aviation maintenance officer (AMO), the administrative officer (S1) and the logistics officer (S4). All other billets within those departments are considered collateral duties and are filled by the lieutenants. Captains fill some lesser department head billets such as NATOPS officer, aviation safety officer (ASO), intelligence officer (S2), assistant operations officer (AOps O) and assistant aviation maintenance officer (AAMO).

In 167, we only had three majors available and initially just three captains. The majors were the XO, the Ops O and the AMO. The captains filled the S1, S2, ASO and S4 billets (our other two majors were assigned permanent VIP duty). So our large collection of lieutenants filled all the other billets, major and minor, some very minor roles—for instance, I was initially assigned as the Marine Corps orders officer, a billet normally handled by a junior corporal or lance corporal in the S1 department. Later, I was assigned to assist the ASO, mostly because he had so many reports to write.

Awards writing was an additional duty shared by the lieutenants working in the "Ops" shop. After each flight, the pilot was required to write a summary of where the flight had gone and what had been accomplished. This duty was usually delegated to the copilot in the gunships. If there had been hostile contact, then the "awards committee" would translate the after-action report into an award recommendation. Most of the lieutenants didn't think much about awards, and since we didn't like writing reports, our after-action reports were pretty brief. After all, we were just doing the job we came here to do. Many times, the XO sat on award recommendations if it did not involve a field grade officer.

What this all amounted to was that the lieutenants did most of the flying, which for most of us was between 50 and 80 hours of actual flight time each month. That does not account for the time we spent waiting during "standby" missions or the hours spent briefing, pre-flighting, debriefing, or after-action report writing. Still, we found time to have fun.

There was an intramural flag football league that our squadron participated in. I actually found time to see one game (we lost). A few of our lieutenants played, mostly those who worked in the Ops shop; they were able to finagle enough time off to play along with several of our troops. While the war was going on 24/7, work was done in shifts, usually 12-hour shifts, so there was a day and a night shift. Therefore, some of the guys had time to play. (Crew chiefs usually worked all day and part of the night. I don't know when or where they slept—probably in their bird.) Flag football was the only organized activity that I knew about and the only one depicted in the squadron cruise book (similar to a yearbook). There may have been others, I just wasn't aware.

The "cruise book" was developed and published by Uncle Milty and MA1. They took most of the pictures, added some taken by other pilots during various missions, then convinced Black Jack that they needed to go to Okinawa to get it published. He said OK, but they had to be back

Lt "Uncle Milty" Matthews receiving a pass during an intramural football game.

17. Intramural and Social Activities

in a week. Somewhere along the line, they must have lost track of time because they didn't get back for a little over two weeks.

Marble Mountain Air Facility had a small exchange and a barber shop. The exchange did provide an inch-thick catalog where we could order almost anything (including cars that we could pick up when we got back to the "world"). I ordered a TEAC 4010 tape deck, an amplifier, a reverb deck and four giant Pioneer speakers. They filled up my space in the hooch, and I got Uncle Milty to pick up a bunch of "dubbed" tapes (original artists popular in the late '60s and early '70s and copied to large tape reels) while he was in Okinawa. As it turned out, it was easy to ship everything back to the States when I got my orders home. The barber shop was manned by a Vietnamese barber, and occasionally we found time to get our hair cut.

The most popular recreation activities were the clubs—officers', staff NCOs' and enlisted, all located with a view of the very impressive beach. The officers' club showed a movie each night on the "veranda"—a porch just off the back of the bar with the movie projected on a large screen set up just across the road from the club on the beach side. Drinking was very popular; most drinks were $0.10 except during "Happy Hour" when they were $0.05. Happy Hour went every night from 5:00 p.m. until 9:00 p.m. We were not very conscious of how much we spent since we were paid in "military payment certificates" (MPC). MPC came in all denominations, from a nickel to $20 and looked like "Monopoly money." No wonder we spent it like water. Actually, MPC was an effort to prevent widespread criminal activity in U.S. currency. The bartenders and waitresses were all young Vietnamese women, dressed in traditional clothing. All were attractive and spoke at least limited English, some very good English.

At least once every month, there would be a USO-sponsored band in the O club, usually a Filipino band. They were great at imitating U.S. and British rock bands and were proficient with every current hit tune. When we had a "country" band, the club would be full (actually, the club was full, no matter the band or movie). Country was the only genre that the Filipino bands could not imitate. So when it was country, we knew it would be a U.S. band, usually with a "round-eye" lead singer in a short skirt.

Drinking was the primary form of recreation in the club, and I participated with the best of them. I started out drinking "screwdrivers," a simple drink with vodka and orange juice. At five cents a drink, I was tossing them down with regularity. It wasn't long before I realized that the acid in the orange juice was killing my stomach. The second drawback to screwdrivers was if we were out of country (the Philippines

A USO show at the MMAF officers' club featuring a Filipino band.

comes to mind), you did not get orange juice; you got orange drink in your screwdriver—not the same at all. Eventually, I switched to "Black Russians," vodka and Kahlua, an all-alcohol drink, still only a nickel of Monopoly money during Happy Hour. By midway through the year, I realized I was on the verge of becoming an alcoholic, if not already there. I needed something to slow me down (besides quitting). I switched to Scotch; now, there is a drink that you have to sip slowly. Many years later, while on deployment to NAS Yeovilton, England, I was introduced to a single malt Scotch called Glenfiddich. I certainly learned to enjoy an occasional sip of such a good Scotch.

Reflecting on situations regarding our restrictions, the Lieutenants Protective Association (LPA) was formed. The LPA was not a "union"-type organization; it had no form or function, but we did post things on a flip cart in the ready room that indicated our "give a sh*t" attitude. For instance, the XO talked about doing things within the "parameters." Immediately, "What is a parameter?" was posted on the flip chart, with a multitude of answers, mostly humorous, and a couple of drawings depicting the elusive "parameter." One picture in the cruise book depicted "The Elusive Green Parameter." One of our favorite sayings became, "The only way you can hurt me with a fitness report is to roll it up and stick it in my eye." And "A letter of reprimand is better than no mail at all." Little did we know. Most of us had no idea whether we might make a career out of the Marine Corps, and an adverse "combat" fitness report could certainly "hurt" you. Later, I found that many of us stayed in the Marine Corps, rising to the lofty "field grade" status.

Flying in combat in Vietnam had started out as a "lieutenant's war" and it still was. Most pilots available to carry out the flying assignments were lieutenants. For the senior officers, their primary duty was something other than flying. They went on missions when they had to, but their other duties had to enjoy some priority. We would have liked to see our commanding officer out there flying a little more, but most of us thought the XO was a little dangerous to fly with.

Elmer "Fudd" Davis editing the "Parameters."

The elusive green "Parameter."

18

Bob Hope Entertains the Troops

December brought another aggressive month of flying, with a mixture of VIP, visual reconnaissance (VR), airborne personnel detection (APD), gunship escort for medevac and resupply. There was a heavy mixture of day and night flights for a personal total of almost 70 hours. On one early morning medevac escort, the Phrog took seven hits with the pilot shot in the knee. We expended 21 rockets and 1,000 rounds of machine gun fire into that target. With this accumulation of experience and flight time, a NATOPS check flight for qualification as a PQM had to be in the near future.

On December 6, 1969, we had an aggressive mortar attack on the flight line. We had some ground support equipment damaged, and one helicopter suffered shrapnel damage to the tail boom and one rotor blade. The mortar hit the blacktop just beside and slightly behind the aircraft. One of our tractors had a couple of tires blown out. Fortunately, the rockets staged nearby were not hit or damaged.

Later in the December 1969 time frame, we had a major change in our table of organization/table of equipment. HML-367, call sign "Scarface" which was operating out of Phu Bai, moved from Phu Bai to Marble Mountain and gained a new aircraft, the AH-1G Cobra, a two-pilot aircraft designed solely as a gunship. They transferred their UH-1E aircraft and many of their pilots to us. The aircraft we gained were a mixture of gunships and slicks (unarmed aircraft). Most of their gunships were equipped with the TAT-101E, which was a transversable weapons system that consists of twin M-60 machine guns mounted under the nose of the aircraft.

The weapon had an aiming system mounted in the cockpit in front of and slightly above the copilot. That weapon provided us with an additional way to confront the enemy. We now had eight M-60 gun

18. Bob Hope Entertains the Troops

Rocket/mortar damage to the tail and blades of TV15.

systems, including the two being operated by the crew chief and gunner, plus our 14-rocket capability.

In some of the cooler months, we experimented with the 19-shot rocket pod which really put us near our max gross weight. At one point during my tour, we worked with some Daisy Cutters, a bomb that would chop down small trees and brush in the landing zone at about four inches height in a radius of about 30 meters. We could carry four of these on bomb racks on each side

Lt Randy Crew in front of a Huey with the TAT-101E armament system.

of the aircraft in place of the rocket pods. The 19-shot pod and the Daisy Cutters are shown in some of the pictures.

This brought our total number of aircraft to around 44, six of them were held in reserve and the rest used daily. The number of pilots assigned to HML-167 grew temporarily to nearly 80 and we were now the only Marine operator of UH-1 slicks in Vietnam, which could be used to support various VIP missions.

Over the next couple of months, HMM-161, call sign "Cattlecall," moved to the west side of Marble Mountain from Phu Bai, followed by HMM-262, call sign "Chatterbox," on February 15. Now all Marine helicopters were operating out of Marble. VMO-6 flying the OV-10 moved to Kadena AFB, and VMO-2 returned to the States. Now there was no Marine aviation presence north of the Hai Van Pass.

As Christmas approached, we pulled one slick out of service, painted it fire engine red with a white top with sculpted lower edges. It was decorated on the main airframe with white stars, and the tail boom was red with a white candy stripe. For several days before Christmas, this aircraft was used to deliver ice cream and gift packages to troops in the field.

Christmas at Marble Mountain was a festive event. The officers' club had a long bar on the ocean side, a large stage opposite the bar and a seating area in between with multiple long tables for unit drink fests. For Christmas, each side of the stage was decorated with a large Christmas tree.

The Christmas Huey launching.

18. Bob Hope Entertains the Troops 87

Early on Christmas Eve, there was a Christmas party for a large group of orphans at the officers' club at Marble Mountain. The red Huey delivered "Santa" to the club for the party. The club was packed with dignitaries, both local and USMC as well as representatives of the American Red Cross.

Later in the day, also on Christmas Eve, we gathered in the O club for a few, which turned into many. A couple of the lieutenant colonel squadron commanders decided to have a tennis ball can gun fight. They cut the ends out of several beer cans, taped them together and poked a small hole near one end. Holding it like a bazooka and by squirting a small amount of lighter fluid in the hole, then igniting it, a tennis ball could be fired from the long string of cans at the target. Empty beer cans were stacked in a pyramid on a table between the Christmas trees, and the fight was on.

After several rounds of firing tennis balls, the target beer cans stood unmolested, but both Christmas trees were destroyed. Knowing the colonels were never going to hit the target, a friend of mine from flight school, a lieutenant nicknamed "Pig," whose family was involved with Ronrico rum, launched himself at the target. He dived through the beer cans, hooked his toes on the edge of the table, performing a perfect "carrier qualification."

The 1969 Christmas party at the O club for the orphans, waiting for "Santa."

Santa arriving at the O club.

During the week between Christmas and New Year, we supported the Bob Hope USO show with our candy cane–painted Huey. The show featured Bob Hope, Neil Armstrong and Ann Margaret and the Gold Diggers, among others. It was presented in an amphitheater near Wing and Division Headquarters west of Da Nang AFB. It was a great show attended by thousands of troops.

We flew Bob Hope, Neil Armstrong and Ann-Margret to several locations near Da Nang for additional shows, then on to Phu Bai for a show there. I attended the show in Da Nang and was seated in the "nosebleed" area of the amphitheater. The candy-striped aircraft was soon returned to its soft green coloring and quickly put back in service.

A few days into the New Year, our squadron officers held a squadron dinner at an air force–sponsored club in Da Nang called the Stone Elephant. This club was famous (at least in our part of the world) for the quality of its steak dinners and high-quality wine. We all rode over in a bus. As we walked into the club, we noted a sign that prohibited the carrying of weapons in the club. We were all wearing the 1969 version of jungle utilities which had a loose-fitting blouse (jacket), perfect for concealing a shoulder holster with weapon underneath. There was no way this large group of Marine officers was going to be unarmed in a war zone and not on base. I can't remember ever being unarmed in Vietnam except for when I took a shower or was asleep in my rack (bed)—my weapon was nearby even then.

18. Bob Hope Entertains the Troops

HML-167 Hueys arriving with Bob Hope for the Christmas show in Da Nang.

The Gold Diggers performing with the Bob Hope show.

After a fantastic dinner with great steaks and good wine and probably lots of other liquor, we hatched a plan to "borrow" the wicker elephant that was displayed in front of the club. As these plans were created, we were quite loud and probably overheard by the staff in the club. This would go down as the only time in history (or maybe one of the few) that the air force thwarted the Marines. We failed miserably, probably due to copious amounts of alcohol imbibed just prior to the attempt, and HML-167 ended up with a lifetime ban from the Stone Elephant.

Fudd was flying a test hop the night we went to the Stone Elephant. So he missed out on some fun. As it turned out, he had his own fun. As he tells the story:

> It had been a long day, and the squadron was having a party off base (a rare event). However, I was approached by a crew chief who had been working on an aircraft all day and the bird was ready for a check flight. There had been rotor-head work, so the first portion of the flight was balancing and tracking the rotor blades. It was now dark, and as the engine had been changed, there was a requirement for an engine vibration check. The necessary equipment had been loaded and connected electrically to the engine. The first portion of the flight was uneventful. A portion of the check flight required an autorotation. I had been flying in a westerly direction south of Monkey Mountain [Monkey Mountain was northeast of Marble Mountain airfield] to avoid any interference with fixed-wing aircraft. I had noted the surf as phosphorous; it was clearly visible. I heard a noise, sort of a huffing sound, checked the EGT [exhaust gas temperature], noted it was around 900 degrees; the max is 620 degrees. We were in a descent as part of the test and were only 300 or 400 feet above the ground. Knowing there was a local cemetery in the black void below, I started a tight left turn back to the beach, while calling the tower, informing them of my situation. I ran the throttle beep switch full forward, the last image from the EGT was over 1,000 degrees. As we cleared the army's 95th Hospital, I continued the turn to line up heading north along the beach directly above the surf. At that moment, a decision had to be made. The local fishermen had their boats pulled up on the sand, so it was either into the boats or the surf. The surf won out, and at that moment the engine quit. I made an immediate pull on the collective and hard rudder to arrest the aircraft spin. We were a heavy gunship, and we impacted the water which was about 18 inches deep under the foam. The crew chief jumped out while I was talking to the tower, who said they could see my red rotating beacon. The crew chief said we were on fire, but it turned out it was just the bright glow from the overheated engine. I was watching three Vietnamese fishermen who were backlit by a blue wall. We were concerned that everyone was friendly since neither of us had a weapon—one of the only times we were completely unarmed.
>
> A CH-53 picked the aircraft up later and brought it back to Marble, where

18. Bob Hope Entertains the Troops

the sand was removed from the belly and the engine and the skids were changed. Once that was complete, the aircraft was sent to Japan for repair.

Just before the end of my tour, I was told to get my helmet, get in the Huey waiting by the hangar and ride over to Da Nang cargo area at Da Nang AFB. When I arrived at Da Nang, I found the Huey freshly painted, I was told to take her home. So ended the test flight, interrupted by a hard landing on a dark night, a major overhaul and a return to a bright sunny flight line, months later.*

Whenever we were able, our squadron partied hard. Bosses' night at the E club was no exception. Most of our senior officers avoided this informal interaction with the "troops," but the LPA was well represented. At one such event, Uncle Milty, and not for the first time, took the stage with Lt Bob Castle and did the "hand jive" on Bob's broad posterior. It is amazing that some of these details can be recalled, considering the quantity of alcohol that was consumed.

One of the lieutenants in our squadron was so good at consuming

MAG-16 enlisted club.

---

* As related to the author by Lt Elmer Davis via email, February 20, 2024.

alcohol that he managed to get a DUI every place we were assigned, TBS at Quantico, Ft. Wolters, Hunter army airfield in Savannah, Oceanside, California, while qualifying in the Huey and in Da Nang when he borrowed (stole) a jeep assigned to one of the general officers there. Many years later, he was killed during a test flight while working for Sikorski Aircraft. He was the lieutenant who had attempted an extended conversation with the young lady in the after-hours club in Dallas I described earlier.

19

Rest and Relaxation

Sydney, Australia, January 1970

January brought a relief from flying with field grade officers and a significant increase in gunship flights. I flew 71 hours in 16 flights with only 1 VIP flight and 1 gunship flight with a captain, no majors.

During a tour in Vietnam, aircrews got four trips out of country. The first was always to Cubi Point Naval Air Station for JEST. The second trip was for seven days of R&R—free vacation (leave), not charged. The third was seven days charged as leave. The fourth trip was four days in Udorn, Thailand, for crew rest. The choices for R&R and leave included Sydney, Hong Kong, Singapore, Taipei and Hawaii. However, the Hawaii visits were reserved primarily for married Marines to rendezvous with their spouses. Travel to most locations was via our old favorite, Tiger Airlines, and was free; your only cost was hotel, meals and booze at your destination. Travel to Thailand was by Marine C-117 (the military version of the old Douglas DC-3). The trips for R&R, JEST, and crew rest did not count as leave.

I chose Sydney and was scheduled to go on R&R from January 26 through February 2, 1970. I had two years of Latin in middle school and a year of French in college. I didn't think either of these would be much help wherever I went, so I figured I should go somewhere I could speak the language. Boy, was I confused! It took me a while to begin to understand the accent and dialect; the words were the same ones I used, but it didn't sound like it.

Australia (at least the part I saw—I did not get out of Sydney) is a beautiful country. The people are friendly, and the beer was cold. I was not a beer fan (and I'm still not), but I gave it a good run. We were given a ride from the airport to a recommended hotel and told where to be seven days hence. From that point on, I was on my own. The hotel clerk recommended a club where most people on R&R and leave ate and drank, and that's where I headed.

Once properly lubricated, I made the discovery that many of the Australian males preferred to hang out with each other, hunt, drink copious amounts of beer and ignore the women. My good fortune. I hadn't been hunting in years, didn't really like the taste of beer but enjoyed the hell out of the company of women.

The club had a large dance area with many young ladies dancing with each other, an adequate bar and a very loud band. The noise interfered with communication, but the ladies seemed to love my abuse of their version of the English language.

I met a nice redhead who spent the next several days showing me around Sydney, the opera house, the gardens and the beach. January in Australia is the middle of the summer (below the equator), but the weather was uncharacteristically cool. We visited the beach, but the wind was blowing and the temperature low, so all we did was visit. Getting into a bathing suit and testing the water was not an option.

Each evening, we (the redhead and I) went back to the club, had a few drinks, ate, danced a few dances and the next thing I knew, my seven days were up and I was boarding the bus back to the airport.

When I got back to the squadron, I heard about one of the Phrog squadron commanding officers who came back from Australia with a couple of black eyes and a couple of stitches in his head. The story he told was that he forgot that Australians drove on the left side of the road (like in England) and that he looked the wrong way, stepped into the street in front of a bus and got hit. The lieutenant grape vine claimed that he approached a young lady without the best intentions in mind, and her boyfriend thumped him. Believe what you may, but my money is with the lieutenants.

Shortly after returning from Sydney, I learned that one of our lieutenants was getting a flight disciplinary board (known in flight school as a "speedy board"), the purpose of which was to remove him from flight status for being too aggressive. (Remember the restrictions the senior officers thought we should follow.) This was the lieutenant whom I flew my first gunship hop with, who told me that most of what our XO briefed about flying guns was BS. The senior member was to be LtCol P. C. Scagloine, commanding officer of HMM-364, the Purple Foxes, call sign Swift.

At the conclusion of the board, LtCol Scagloine and the board found no justification to remove the lieutenant from flight status and instead offered him a transfer to HMM-364. The latter went on to win a Distinguished Flying Cross for his work as a copilot rescuing a crew from a downed HMM-262 aircraft.*

---

* Walker, Harold G., *The Grotto*, Book Two, Dragonfly Publishing, 165–169, citation 451.

20

Control Problems

My first flight in February started off with a bang—actually, several of them. We launched at 0700 and didn't complete until 1900 that day. We were flying gunship escort for some Phrogs doing recon inserts in several locations. We took fire from the enemy on three separate occasions and returned same. After several hours of inserts, DASC diverted us to Mission 80, which was gunship escort for a rapid reaction force. They had identified over 100 Vietcong/North Vietnamese Army (VC/NVA) in some trees near Hill 55. Our task was to insert a blocking force while elements from the regiment swept through the area. We took more fire from the VC and expended 24 rockets and about 6,000 rounds of machine gun fire.

I had gunship flights on February 4, 6 and 8–14, with plenty of contact and opportunities to shoot rockets and guns at the enemy. In my spare time over the last week or so, I completed my closed-book exams for qualification in the aircraft. On the 13th, I had medevac escort flight as a copilot to our AMO, who was a pretty good major. During the flight, we had four separate flights into bad-guy country where we evacuated four separate Marines with critical injuries. We didn't have any enemy contact on this flight, which allowed time for the AMO to put me through the paces in the aircraft. I thought this was an excellent warm-up for a check ride, but the major wrote it up as my NATOPS check. Three days later, I had my first flight in charge of the aircraft. Finally, PQM!

My first flight on February 17 as a PQM was an uneventful four hours in support of the ROK Marines (Mission 7). I wasn't by myself; I had another copilot who got in country in early December. We transported 18 passengers to a number of landing zones in the area south of Da Nang. On the 18th, my second PQM flight wasn't quite so bland.

There is no good time for control problems in an aircraft of any type, airplane, helicopter, balloon, glider or rocket. Some are just worse than others! Close to the ground falls into one of the worst, if not the worst, time for things to go wrong.

Before going into detail about this experience, I'm putting on my longtime aviation safety officer hat and editorialize about how to handle such emergencies.

The first thing to do in any emergency is FLY THE DAMN AIRCRAFT! More people have killed themselves and everybody with them by troubleshooting the emergency while flying into the ground instead of first flying the aircraft. Checklists for emergencies should be memorized, then followed while you fly! I cannot count the number of accident investigations I participated in over the next 23 years whose impact could have been lessened by first flying the aircraft. Now, what happened with my aircraft.

Once fully qualified and oriented, you are on your own. After a little while, you get to train the next FNG (f**king new guy). Most of the time (all, if you wanted to stay alive), you wore a lot of equipment when flying. Flight suit, boots and helmet were normal, plus a web belt with a sidearm—aviators carried a .38 revolver, plus a survival vest and on top of that we added a ceramic plate in a vest rated to stop a .50 caliber round. One of our guys had tested that theory when a .50 caliber round came through his cockpit, striking him in the chest plate. It worked—sort of; he still got temporarily medevac'd, but he lived through it and was returned to flight status the same month.

The vest also had a back plate, which we usually took out and put in the chin bubble of the aircraft to provide additional protection from small-arms fire for the cockpit area. Both pilot seats were armored and provided protection from the outboard side, bottom (I would test this later) and back. The crew chief and gunner wore both the front and back plates in their vests as they had no other protection.

Seat adjustments in the Huey, to accommodate pilots of different stature, were pretty simple. The seats could be raised about ten inches, so short pilots could see over the cockpit panel; they also had a fore and aft adjustment range of about eight or ten inches for short- or long-armed crew members. The pedals also had a fore and aft range for short or long legs. I'm a short guy, so I usually adjusted my seat about halfway forward and halfway up, then I brought the foot pedals as far aft as they would go. I assume that most people of similar stature did the same thing.

The mission where I had my control problems was a simple flight; I had an FNG with me, a friend from Basic School, Al. Al was about the same height as I am, near five feet eight inches; however, it was a lot further around his waist and he wore *all* the proscribed equipment. Al was not fat; he was just a big guy, very strong.

20. Control Problems

Al was assigned the nickname Big Al. Al had been an army paratrooper before attending college at Southeast Missouri State College. While there, he participated in the platoon leaders course, a two-summer training session at Marine Corps Base, Quantico, Virginia, that led to commissioning as a second lieutenant in the Marines upon graduation from college. After commissioning, he was assigned to TBS and was in the same training company as me. After completion of TBS, he attended the army flight training program a few weeks behind me. He arrived in country in late December 1969.

The mission was simple: we were to pick up a greeting party for an arriving Korean general at III MAF headquarters, then transport the escort to Da Nang AFB to greet the general. Later, we would take them both to the Korean base just south of Marble Mountain Airfield. Additionally, he would get a VR of the Korean operating area before we returned him to Da Nang AFB. Our base, Marble Mountain Air Facility, was located just south and east of Da Nang AFB.

We planned our arrival at Da Nang early to give me the opportunity to show Al the routing in and out of Da Nang AFB and allow us some time to fly the pattern and for him to get a little "stick time" before we had to make our pickup. We would do some additional area orientation after the drop, including routes into the VIP pads north and west of Da Nang city. I made the first approach to Da Nang AFB, maintaining 60 knots indicated airspeed, until we were midway down the 10,000-foot runway and within about 50 or so feet of the ground. I eased the cyclic back to begin slowing the aircraft, and bang, the cyclic wouldn't come back past neutral! Oh crap! Too close to the ground, too fast! Here's where **flying the aircraft first** comes into play. I figured the best place to troubleshoot this problem was somewhere farther away from the ground; inadvertent ground contact at or above 60 knots would not be good and would probably be called a crash landing—didn't want that! So I added power, told Da Nang tower I was going around and began climbing. The second thing to do in an emergency is communicate. I told Da Nang I was having some control problems and needed some altitude to check them out.

Once a little further airborne, I moved the cyclic a little forward, then pulled it back; I moved it only a little—didn't want it stuck any further forward. As I pulled back, it stopped about the same place that it had before. I tried again, this time moving it further forward, then back. The forward movement was unrestricted, and I could always pull it back to the same spot. Holding the cyclic firmly aft, I looked at Al to ask what he thought. As I looked at him, I realized that his seat was full up and full forward. As I pulled the cyclic back, I could see it was hitting on his ceramic plate; there was no way to slow this aircraft with his seat in that position. Now I knew the problem. However, to solve this problem, he needed longer arms and legs or less circumference, neither of which would happen quickly!

For an immediate solution, I had him fly with his seat lower and further back and suggested he bring the pedals to the full aft position. He had gotten comfortable with the previous seat position at Hunter and reinforced it at Camp Pendleton while training there; however, he had not been wearing body armor and full survival gear then. Once his seat was adjusted, we had no further problems and were able to complete our mission successfully. The Korean general never knew that there had been a problem and got to review the Korean forces without incident. After dropping the general at his headquarters, we continued our orientation of the area and had a couple of good laughs about our situation. I promised Al I wouldn't mention the problem to anyone else, and I am sure he was able to find a comfortable seat adjustment after this flight.

To the best of my knowledge, Big Al had a successful tour. I did have an opportunity to fly with Big Al several times over the next seven months and know he had a successful year. After completing his Marine obligations, Al returned to the army and flew for many more years. I still see some posts from him on Facebook and in Pop-A-Smoke.com occasionally.

From the 18th through the 27th, I flew mostly single-pilot VIP missions with a couple of dual-pilot hops in support of Mission 7 thrown in. On the 28th, I got my first PQM gunship hop flying medevac escort out of LZ Baldy. This almost-five-hour flight had 9 emergency medevacs and 14 priority medevacs out of seven zones, including one pickup that our lead gunship accomplished when the Phrogs could not locate the landing zone. At one site, we took fire from the enemy and returned fire with rockets and guns until the enemy fire was suppressed. I finished this month with over 72 hours flown.

21

Lost Camera

One of our standard missions (Mission 7) was flown in support of the ROK Marines. The mission profile called for a slick Huey flown single pilot with a crew chief and chased by a CH-46. Usually, the only passengers were a senior officer from the Korean regiment with a couple of "strap hangers" (the entourage of butt kissers who followed someone senior to them, hoping to gain favor), in which case, the Phrog just followed us around in case something went wrong.

The ROK Marines were and are famous for their fierce fighting capabilities and their lack of sympathy for their enemies. What is lesser known is their adherence to a strict and violent discipline. Junior Marines would receive a severe beating for simple violations of protocol or regulations, and they did not ever dare to fight back. There were no excuses allowed; violation equals a beating, and there were damn few violations. Sometimes these beatings were in sequence, with an officer beating a staff non-commissioned officer, who then beat a junior enlisted man. Stuff does roll downhill, especially in the ranks of the Korean Marines.

Today's mission was going to be a little different; we would proceed to ROK headquarters, pick up a couple of officers in the Huey and a squad of ROK Marines in the '46, take and drop them at China Beach to do a little shopping, then return to the Land of the Blue Dragon (ROK headquarters), pick up the regimental Ops O and a couple of others take them to Hill 55 for a meeting with the regimental ops there. From there, they would go to LZ Baldy for another meeting, then return them to ROK headquarters. Finally, we would go back to China Beach to pick up and return the shopping squad to the Land of the Blue Dragon. At that point, we would be done for the day and would be released to return to Marble. Total flight time would be about four hours, maybe four and a half, with probably three hours of wait time. We would have to sneak in a refueling or two somewhere in there.

After making contact with the crew from HMM-364, call sign Swift (364's squadron area adjoined 167's, so briefing and coordination was fairly easy), we conducted our brief and pre-flight. Once we had verified all was in readiness, we cranked up and launched. When clear of Marble, we contacted Swift on the pre-briefed frequency and rendezvoused with the Phrog south of Marble. Continuing south along Highway 1, we contacted the ROK headquarters and reported about five minutes out. Our radio contact with the ROK Marines was always conducted through GySgt Lee; he was probably the best English speaker there. He said the crew going to China Beach was standing by and would be ready to board immediately.

After loading the squad, we headed north on Highway 1, swinging west while south of Da Nang AFB, then north around the west side of the city, with a quick right turn into China Beach. These hardworking ROK Marines could enjoy their hard-earned shopping day in the largest exchange in the Far East. Now we could get to work supporting the movement of the ROK leadership, while they met with their U.S. Marine counterparts.

When we returned to the ROK site, the Ops O and his assistant were ready to go. So we loaded up and headed to Hill 55 for the first stop. After we unloaded, it was a short hop over to An Hoa airfield for a quick refueling, then return to Hill 55 where we would shut down and wait for the meeting to conclude.

Hill 55, Southern I Corps, RVN.

21. Lost Camera

The one-hour meeting went about an hour and a half, so we were alert and ready when the passengers arrived. The start sequence for the Huey is fairly quick, while the Phrog takes just a few minutes more. As soon as we had our engine cranked and the '46 had its auxiliary power plant online, we contacted them by radio and continued our run-up, slowing our procedures just enough so that we were ready to go simultaneously with our chase aircraft.

With everybody aboard, it was off to Baldy for another drop and wait. We got clearance through the TAOR from HDC and proceeded. As we proceeded through the TAOR, there was a football-shaped island in the river that we always avoided because of the high concentration of VC hidden in the tunnel complex. The actual name of the island was Goi Noi island, but we referred to is as "No Go" island.

Upon landing and shutdown, we were met by escorts for the Koreans, who quickly departed for their meeting. If I were smarter, I would have had some books sent to me just for these occasions. Eventually, the meeting concluded. We loaded our passengers and headed back to the Korean landing zone.

After dropping the leadership at their home landing zone, we got clearance from HDC and headed north to pick up the squad we had left at China Beach, with a quick stop at Marble Mountain to top off our fuel tanks. We departed Marble Mountain to the west, and once we were clear of the Da Nang AFB corridor, we turned north to China Beach.

Goi Noi Island known as NO GO island.

LZ Baldy Southern I Corps, RVN.

Arriving there, we found our squad ready and waiting their transportation back to their base.

We dropped the squad at the Land of the Blue Dragon and were cleared to return to Marble, mission complete for the day. As soon as we departed, we went to the pre-briefed common frequency and immediately got a call from our Swift chase bird, who reported that his crew chief was missing his Cannon SLR 35 mm camera. I immediately reported the missing camera to GySgt Lee at landing zone control at the ROK headquarters and got the response, "Call me back in 15."

Swift and I entered an orbit just west of the zone, waiting until we could call back.

Fifteen minutes later, I called, "Blue Dragon LZ, Comprise 11, checking on the status of our missing camera."

"Comprise 11, Blue Dragon LZ," came the reply, "I have the camera. Come back and I will meet you in the LZ."

"Blue Dragon, Comprise, roger, inbound."

Swift dropped into the zone, retrieved the camera and we all returned to Marble. We did not ask the status of the person who had the camera; we knew that he was probably recovering from some recent injuries, probably suffered in close combat with the enemy.

22

Dings on the Tail Rotor

In the middle of 1968, when I was in TBS, the Marine Corps had a very high demand for pilots. To satisfy that requirement, a portion of aviation-qualified officers were sent to either the U.S. Air Force or the U.S. Army flight training programs. To be sent to one of these special assignments, you had to be flight qualified and one of the top academic performers in your class at TBS. The officer sent to interview and sign us to our contracts was a major, A-4 pilot from the training branch of headquarters, U.S. Marine Corps.

As any former Marine knows, you are constantly running into other Marines whom you have known before, in airports, in bars and sometimes at your next assignment. That turned out to be the case for me; as I checked into HML-167 for my tour in Vietnam, I learned that our XO was none other than the major who had signed me to the aviation contract for flight school. He was one of several field grade fixed-wing pilots who were being involuntarily transitioned into helicopters to satisfy the shortage of field grade helicopter pilots in Vietnam. I tried not to see much of the good major as most of us junior lieutenants attempted to avoid contact with or being required to report to the senior field grade officers.

On one stormy night, the sky was obscured with alcohol, we (the LPA) managed to rearrange some (a lot) of sandbags from where they were to a pile located conspicuously in front of the major's door to his hooch. Eventually, another major, or possibly a group of majors, released him.

Our squadron had two types of aircraft assigned, slicks and guns. The slicks had no aircraft mounted armament and were used primarily for VIP support and some command and control. When I first arrived in Vietnam, our gunships had four forward-firing fixed-mount M-60 machine guns, two fixed-mount seven-shot 2.75-inch folding-fin aerial rocket pods and two crew-served M-60s that had a sweeping range of fire, fore and aft, up and down. Later, we got several aircraft that also had a TAT-101E (twin M-60s) mounted under the nose and operated by the copilot as an aimable, transversable weapon.

The links that hold the "belt" of bullets and the shell casings for the crew-served weapons were captured in bags mounted on the guns, but for the fixed-mount weapons, the links and shell casings were ejected outboard from the aircraft.

The aiming system for the Huey gunships is very delicate and required a soft touch from the pilots to be effective. Part of the system was a "plus" sign painted on the windscreen right in front of the pilots. The second part was a folding arm mounted above the windscreen with an open circle mounted on the end. Through the circle, safety wire formed a cross, which frequently got "adjusted."

To aim your missiles and guns, you flew the aircraft in a slight to moderate dive, with a little power pulled (slightly raising the collective), ball centered and align the mark on the windscreen with the fold down site, squeeze the trigger and hope to hit the earth. If the "ball" (indicating aircraft balance) was out of center, not only did the rockets not go where you wanted them; the links and shell casings from the left-side fixed-mount guns would strike the tail rotor, damaging the blades and requiring several hours' labor to replace them (if there were any blades in the supply system).

Fold-down sight and cross of the Huey aiming system.

22. Dings on the Tail Rotor

Pilots flying fixed-wing aircraft usually did not have to deal with "ball" issues, but in helicopters, ball control, done with rudders, was one of the necessary elements of flying the aircraft. As one of our only fixed-wing converts, our XO had significant issues with rudder control; in fact, many of the crews reported that the only time he had the ball in the center was when it passed through from one of the extremes to the other. Therefore, on most of his gunship flights, maintenance crews had to replace tail rotor blades afterward.

Crew chiefs live to fly; they hate spending time doing unnecessary maintenance on their aircraft. Together, they devised an answer for the problem. Although they weren't able to improve the major's flying skills, they did prevent any further damage to their tail rotors. Whenever the major had an opportunity to shoot, the belts feeding ammunition to the left-side guns somehow managed to develop a "kink" preventing the advancement of bullets to the guns. Without bullets to the guns, no links or shell casings were flying overboard, and no damage was inflicted on the tail rotors.

I don't think the XO ever figured out why his left-side guns never worked; he just continued to write a maintenance discrepancy on the aircraft. Those discrepancies were eventually signed off as "A799" (maintenance speak for "could not duplicate").

23

Night Fright or Which Way Is Up?

Night flight before the advent of night-vision goggles was always a trial. You learned to pick out clues to orient yourself. Helicopters (and airplanes) have running lights to help your positioning: red on the left side of the aircraft and green on the right, a small white light on the tail. The anti-collision light is a flashing red light and bright enough to be seen at a considerable distance. The running lights are dimmer so as to not ruin your "night vision." Another help to night flight is night adaptation, where the only light you are exposed to is a red light for about 30–60 minutes before flight.

Sometimes the natural environment helps maintain your adaptation like when your flight is in remote areas with minimal artificial lighting; sometimes it hurts when your flight remains in a highly illuminated area like near a major city. Airfields themselves have minimal lighting: usually no ramp lights, only blue taxiway lights and white runway lights. The medevac waiting area had soft red lighting inside and no light outside and was in a separate building (hut) away from the majority of airfield operations.

Lt John Gale, Comprise 22, tells a frightening story about one of his flights.

> A couple of months before this flight, two Cobra helicopters had crashed at Marble Mountain airfield. I was flying home from a mission and saw one of the burning aircraft about 100 feet from the fuel pits near our revetments with fire trucks and crash crew controlling the blaze. The two Cobras from our sister squadron had come over the home field to do a formation break. They had closed it up real tight to look good. When the section leader broke, he increased his angle of bank too fast and too much, or his wingman was too close, and their rotors hit. The main rotors of both aircraft separated from the aircraft, and both aircraft fell to the ground killing all four pilots. I

23. Night Fright or Which Way Is Up?

concluded, as I believe every helicopter pilot who ever flew formation does, that if your rotors hit, everybody dies.

The other important observation occurred in the chow line at the Marble Mountain officers' mess. I was standing in a line behind 30 or more lieutenants. The fellow right in front of me, Lt Chuck Steele, Comprise 20, was telling several of us about a flight he had just completed, with great enthusiasm. He was the pilot in command of a Huey in a section of two. The other pilot in command was someone I can still picture, but now I'm not sure of his name. Chuck and the other pilot were returning from a mission and decided to play or practice a dogfight like you would see in the World War I biplane movies.

A Huey gun cruises at about 100 knots, so it's about like a biplane in speed and maneuverability, except you're not supposed to fly it upside down or get it into zero-G flight. The Huey has a semirigid under-slung rotor blade system. If you get it into a zero-G situation, the rotor system becomes undamped, and a quick movement of the controls can create forces on the rotor head and rotor mast and bearings that can cause failure of the system and separation of the main rotor from the aircraft. A no-fun experience!

Chuck said the other Huey was right on his tail, and he was banking right and turning as tight as he could and rolling left, but everything he tried, the pilot stayed right with him. The other pilot was keying his mic and going da-da-da-da-da like he was lacing him with bullets in his wings like the war movies. Chuck then said to us in the chow line, "You can turn a Huey upside down and it won't know it's upside down as long as you keep positive G's on the rotor system." So he rolled it upside down and split S'ed out. I remember his facial expression as he described pulling through the vertical nose down and pulling right through to wings level nose level. He said the other pilot didn't follow him.

We stood night medevac in a little SEA hut right next to the runway. The 46 pilots and crew took one side, and the Huey pilots and crew took the other side. When we got a medevac, the copilots would run out and start the aircraft while the pilots listened to the radio call for any details.

On this one, the pickup zone was just south of the Ca To river bridge and a little back east toward the ocean. We took off from the Marble Mountain Air Facility on the beaches of the South China Sea, east of Da Nang airport, and headed north. We turned west over the Ca To river and low leveled down the river. In keeping with our standard operating procedure, we flew down the river at about 20 feet above the river until we passed the Ca To river bridge so that we would be past the extended center line of the Da Nang runway, and we wouldn't get run over by a jet taking off or landing. After passing the Ca To river bridge, we started our climb to 1,500 feet and turned south.

The coordinates for the pickup LZ were very close, so we went into a left turn within less than a mile from where we had turned south. I think we were at an altitude of 1,500 feet by the time we were abeam the coordinates we were looking for.

The light was different than most night medevacs because we were still close to Da Nang, and there was a lot of light from the air facility and Da Nang in general. It made looking down at the ground seem very dark.

This is when things became unusual. The radio operator on the ground told us that he didn't have a strobe light, that he was using a flashlight and was turning it on and off to get a blinking effect.

I was behind Capt Mike Hammer, Comprise 9, who was pilot in command of the lead Huey. We were in a gentle left turn, and I had him in the center of my side of the windshield so that I was staying on a typical bearing of him for a left turn, and I was a distance back which was normal for night operations. At this point, I was probably about 200 yards behind him, and I had begun increasing the distance between us because we would be maneuvering into a "180 out" position. We normally set up in a right-hand orbit around the position on the ground, with us being opposite one another in a circle, so that when I would look out my right window, he would be at my three o'clock position, or 180 degrees out from me, and about a quarter mile away.

However, at this point, we were in a left turn, over the position, and I thought I saw the blinking flashlight. I was in the right seat, and I saw the light out the left side of the back opening of the helicopter. We flew the gunships with no doors on the back so that the crew chief and gunner could man their swivel-mounted M-60 machine guns and so that they could tend to the four forward-firing M-60s and the seven-shot rocket pods.

I thought I saw the light, so I keyed my intercom switch and told my aircrew that I thought I saw it and described where I thought it was to my crew. Everyone in my aircraft was looking out the left windows, trying to see the light I had seen.

Capt. Hammer, in the lead aircraft, said, "I'm coming back right, John." I said, "Roger," which means I understand, and I will take your lead appropriately so as to stay out of your way. I had rogered him, but it didn't really register in my mind because I was still distracted looking at the ground trying to see the blinking flashlight again.

When I did glance up, Capt. Hammer was still in the same relative position on my windshield, so everything seemed OK. Suddenly, I realized that I was seeing his red running light on my right side and his green running light on my left side. His red light is on the left or port side of the helicopter, and the green is on the right or starboard side of his helicopter.

That meant that we were on a collision course! He was coming at me, not going away. By the time I realized that we were on a collision course, we were so close that it seemed improbable that we wouldn't have a midair collision. The two Cobras crashing at home field, "If our rotors hit, everybody dies" flashed into my mind, and Chuck Steele's "If you keep positive G's, the helicopter doesn't know you are upside down" flashed into my mind simultaneously. I thought, "If I can roll it upside down, our rotors won't hit, and somebody might live!"

It was way less than a second from the time I realized we were on a collision course to the time I pulled the cyclic stick all the way to the right. I had to lift my right foot off the rudder pedal and move my leg out of the way so that I could hit the stops on the cyclic stick to get maximum roll rate to the right. As we rolled through 90 degrees angle of bank, I pulled the collective

23. Night Fright or Which Way Is Up?

pitch to full power and pulled full back stick (cyclic) to get out of his path as fast as possible. I continued to roll until upside down and was diving toward the ground. I saw Mike go by in my chin bubble which was on the bottom of my helicopter just in front of the rudder pedals. He was off to my right and about 20 feet above me when he went by.

I kept positive G's on the helicopter as I rolled to the left to wings level. This was all on instruments because it was dark out, and I had no reliable outside reference. I was about 45 degrees nose down. The UH-1E has a redline airspeed of 140 knots. Helicopters don't stall like airplanes. They can get into retreating blade edge stall if you go too fast or you pull too many G's on a pull out. We passed through 145 knots on the pull out, but I didn't feel any retreating blade edge stall symptoms during the pullout. The main rotor speed (revolutions per minute) had started to over-speed, so I had to roll the throttle down to flight idle and increase collective pitch to keep from over-speeding the rotor as I pulled out to wings level and normal flight attitude. When I got the nose up, I put the power back on and finished breaking my rate of descent. I don't remember what altitude I was at when we leveled out, but we were only at 1,500 feet when we started, so I didn't have a lot of altitude to play with. I turned to the right and found Capt Hammer and got into my proper position in the orbiting circle.

Capt Hammer was a second-tour Marine pilot and a real cool head. He was a pleasure to fly with. He was one of my favorite teachers when I was a copilot. When I had gone by his aircraft, I was just 20 feet below him and a little to his left, no more than 10 or 15 feet, and I was upside down. When I went by him, I doubt that he realized I was upside down.

He said, "Not so close, John" in a cool non-excited voice. At that moment, I was rolling over into an upright position and starting my pullout.

I replied, "Roger" in an equally cool voice (like "I'm cool"). It's the macho game. You got to sound cool no matter how close you just came to killing yourself and seven other people.

No one in my helicopter said a word. No one else said a word. I wonder if the CH-46s that were orbiting at 2,500 feet above us saw how close we came to a midair collision.

When we completed the mission, we returned to Marble Mountain Air Facility and were sitting in the fuel pits refueling with the engine running and rotors turning when my copilot said to me over the intercom system, "John, I thank you and my fiancée thanks you." I don't remember what I said, but I probably said something like, "If we had hit, all eight of us would be dead, and it would have been all my fault."

I am eternally grateful that I heard Chuck Steele's conversation in the chow line about the concept that you can turn the Huey upside down if you keep positive G's on it. That inspired me to roll inverted to ensure our rotors wouldn't hit as I tried to avoid what seemed like an imminent midair.*

---

* As related to the author by Lt John Gale via email, March 14, 2024.

24

Eagle Claw or What Country Is This?

March was a busy and eventful month. I had 24 flights, 17 gunship and 7 single ship, totaling 74.1 hours all sandwiched around a five-day leave in Taipei, Taiwan. Gunship escort was for medevac, resupply, APD, and rapid reaction. There were lots of getting shot at, lots of return fire and lots of nighttime. This was also a difficult month as we lost a couple of aircraft and several personnel to enemy action. On different days this month, we had to ground all the aircraft, first for a "Rockwell hardness" inspection of the tail rotors, and two days later we had to inspect the stabilization bars on the rotor head.

One of the missions we routinely supported was anything but routine. It posted as Mission 72 and was called Eagle Claw. It was launched out of Phu Bai and went west, way west. It was one of those cluster f's that involved more than one country and more than one service. The Marine contribution was a section of gunships that led the flight as mission commander and a couple of sections of AH-1G Cobras from HML-367. There were also Army of the Republic of Vietnam (AVRN) transport aircraft (usually H-34 aircraft), U.S Army escort and intelligence services and the ground troops were Montagnards (a tribe of people indigenous to the mountain regions of northern South Vietnam) and occasionally force recon personnel. To be involved in this mission, you had to sign a non-disclosure agreement that was valid for five years. Although these missions have been declassified, I am not comfortable with detailed descriptions of the specifics, so I will remain vague while discussing this adventure.

The mission was launched early out of Marble Mountain and proceeded to Phu Bai, about 45 or 50 miles north of Da Nang, to meet up with the other elements. Briefing for the mission was done in Phu Bai by an army commander. After matching up with the other elements,

24. Eagle Claw or What Country Is This?

we would refuel and launch to the west. As we neared the western border of Vietnam, we would top off our fuel tanks at a prepositioned site en route. Leaving the refueling point, the flights went radio silent; the rest of the mission would be conducted without further radio contact unless "something" hit the fan. Once the ground forces were inserted, we kept a section of guns on standby at Phu Bai to escort rescue and recovery forces, whose mission was to pull the guys out. If the mission progressed over several days, the gunships and crews would be replaced every day. If the ground forces were detected, they would use the code word "Prairie Fire" when in Laos and "Nickel Steel" if in the Republic of Vietnam to signify there was known enemy contact and they were proceeding to a preplanned extract point. It was important, politically, not to have the mission become common knowledge because of where they were, yet it seemed that everyone (in our squadron and several support squadrons) knew about it.

HML-167 began supporting this mission in December 1969, and our support would continue through June 1970. Several pilots had reported taking 21-mm anti-aircraft fire during these missions, but they continued anyway. On the mission of March 21, 1970, there was heavy enemy contact en route to the insertion point. Lt Mike Smith, Comprise 15, flying with Lt George Leaming, Comprise 48, reports that Lt Bob Castle's aircraft, the lead gunship and mission commander for this insert, was hit by enemy fire on a gun run which created an immediate onboard fire. Bob's aircraft was observed to crash and explode on ground contact. An immediate attempt to locate any survivors was unsuccessful as the crash site was on a hillside. There was no nearby place to land, and rockets and M60 rounds were cooking off at the site. There was no contact on the emergency frequency with any potential survivors.*

The flight, which also included three army UH-1Hs and three ARVN CH-34s, was low fuel by now, and the entire flight returned to Phu Bai. It was the desire of the Marine Corps to return to the location and conduct a more thorough search for survivors and recover any bodies that could be located.

Our desire to return to that area was constantly denied by the army command running the mission, who reported through their intel services that the wreckage had been booby-trapped and that enemy forces were in the area waiting for our return. This went on for 19 days while we continued to fly in support of separate missions in this area. On the day after the shootdown, our commanding officer, Black Jack, flew his one and only Eagle Claw mission.

---

* As related to the author by Col Mike Smith via email, March 20, 2024.

On the 22nd, I left for a few days' leave in Taipei, Taiwan. I did not do much while there: just slept in, hit a few bars and did a little bit of sightseeing. On the day I returned from Taipei, two of the Cobras from HML-367, while conducting a midfield break, had a midair collision and crashed into the fuel pits at Marble Mountain. All four pilots were killed in the mishap (aviation safety talk describing an accident).

Normally, when conducting a "break," the aircraft are in either a left or right echelon. If the aircraft are in a left echelon—that is, the aircraft are aligned to the left rear of the lead aircraft—then the break is to the right in sequence with the second aircraft breaking about two seconds after the lead aircraft. If there are more than two aircraft in the formation, each aircraft breaks about two seconds after the aircraft in front of them.

In this case, the lead aircraft broke into the echelon instead of away from it, with the expected result. The debris from the midair landed in the fuel pits and caused a subsequent fire.

Nineteen days after our aircraft was shot down, another insert mission to be conducted by the army was planned for an area slightly farther west. As the flight of ten army Hueys flew over a clearing just west of the earlier crash site and continuing west, one of the crew members in the number 10 aircraft reported seeing what looked like someone in a flight suit waving something near the clearing. The aircraft came around for another pass and confirmed that there was what appeared to be someone in flight clothing on the edge of the clearing.

As the aircraft began an approach to the zone, a lightly bearded Caucasian came running out of the tree line, waving a plastic map and being chased by some enemy soldiers. A gunship in the flight laid down some fire behind the fleeing Marine, inhibiting the enemy's plans to capture him, and the aircraft on the ground used the door-mounted machine guns to fire at the enemy while the American ran to and leaped aboard the aircraft. After escaping the zone, it was determined that the rescued airman was the copilot from the previously crashed Marine gunship. The entire flight then returned to Phu Bai with the rescuee. After landing, the army crew counted 34 bullet holes in their aircraft; fortunately, nothing vital was hit and there were no casualties. A couple of Marine pilots from 167 who knew the copilot were flown to Phu Bai to positively identify him.

During the debriefing, the young Marine lieutenant revealed that when his aircraft was hit by enemy fire, the pilot flying was attempting a controlled landing. As the aircraft was descending, the copilot noted that there was a clearing that would work for an extraction landing zone on the next hill west of where they were about to crash land.

The location of the potential extraction point was communicated to the rest of the crew in case they were separated. Fire was raging through the aircraft, and my friend had unbuckled his seat belt to escape some of the flames.

When the aircraft hit the ground, he was thrown forward through the windscreen and landed some distance from the aircraft. He reported that although there was intense enemy fire in the area, he attempted to move closer to the burning aircraft to check for other survivors. He couldn't immediately locate any survivors, although he did find the pilot and noted that he was dead. Because of the enemy rifle fire, he started moving west toward the next hilltop.

After clearing the crash site, he found a sheltered area where he could conceal himself. Moving only at night he said that it took him several days to get down the hillside where they had crashed and up to the next hilltop. The only survival gear he had was his pistol, a few pen flairs and a large plastic-covered map, which he used as a blanket when he rested. His survival vest and bullet bouncer (ceramic vest) never made it out of the aircraft since he wasn't wearing them at the time of the crash. For the next ten days, he stayed near the crest of the hill close to the potential landing zone, leaving only to gather a few berries and to drink from a nearby stream. He saw several enemy patrols but was able to avoid contact, although he did hear gunfire. Twice he saw a flight of helicopters that were some distance away; he fired the pencil flares hoping to attract their attention but without success.

When he saw the army flight of helicopters going over his area, he attempted to signal them by waving his map; he thought they were looking for him instead of doing another insert. He was exhausted and at the end of his rope. His daytime movement attracted the attention of some nearby enemy. As the aircraft neared the ground, he broke cover and ran toward the aircraft. This was his last chance. His dash toward safety then brought on a full-blown chase by the enemy. He was extracted on April 9, 1970, the same day as the 167 change of command.

His medical exam revealed several deep cuts on his shoulder and arm that he had kept wrapped as best he could, although the wounds had gotten maggots in them. During recovery, the doctors said that by ignoring the maggots and keeping the wounds wrapped with pieces of his torn flight suit, he probably saved his arm. He required several surgeries to treat his wounds and remove all the maggots.

With his rescue, the Marine Corps decided that we were going back to the crash site to attempt to recover any bodies that remained. The recovery flight was put together without any other service involvement and consisted of two Huey gunships to lead the flight, four Marine

Cobras to escort, two Marine CH-46's to insert the recovery team, a Marine CH-53 Sea Stallion with an external load crew to recover the damaged aircraft if possible and a single UH-1E slick aircraft with a hoist to lift out anybody as needed. I was tapped to fly the slick with Tom Broderick and a crew chief to handle the hoist. During briefing, I calculated that even though we would be low fuel, at that altitude we would only be able to lift a couple of additional people. I sincerely hoped this would go smoothly.

The flight to Phu Bai was uneventful. We refueled, re-briefed and prepped for launch. After launch, we flew west to the first refueling point; we were the last aircraft to top our tanks. From this point west, it was radio silent. The tension (in our aircraft at least) was high. I was flying in the left seat; the hoist was mounted on the right side. The crew chief would operate the hoist from the right side, and if we had any significant weight on the hoist, lateral center of gravity could be a problem. The crew chief and I were keeping a constant lookout for any sign of enemy activity. Arriving over the crash site, the lead Phrog made a death spiral approach to insert the search and recovery team. After dropping the insert team, he pulled out to an overhead orbit while the ground team did their work. The guns widened their orbit to watch for enemy activity; we remained at altitude in an orbit short of the zone hoping we would not be called on and the recovery effort would be successful. If we were needed, the crap had really hit the fan.

The ground crew reported that they had recovered the body of the pilot; there was no sign of the crew, and there was not enough of the crashed aircraft left to recover. They estimated that the bodies of the aircrew were probably buried under the remains of the aircraft and some heavy-duty digging equipment would be required to remove the wreckage. They found no booby traps, and no enemy activity was noted. The Phrog was cleared back into the zone to recover the body and the ground crew, and we were quickly on the way back to Phu Bai. I don't know today if the bodies of the crew have ever been recovered.

Bravo Zulu to 1stLt Larry Parsons (the copilot) for the execution of his SERE plan. As a side note, I visited Larry in the army medical facility where he was being treated before being evacuated back to the States. He told me he hadn't had a drink since he was rescued, so I sneaked him out and took him to an army club on the west side of the airfield. Nobody ever figured that out; it remains our secret. I noted recently in the *Semper Fidelis* newsletter that Larry had passed on. Rest in peace, old friend.

Lt Paul Pratt, the wing intelligence briefing officer and SERE coordinator, reported this from a debriefing with the copilot, Lt Larry Parsons:

24. Eagle Claw or What Country Is This?

I debriefed Larry Parsons on the incident where Bob Castle (the aircraft commander) and Larry (the copilot) were covering an extraction from Laos and were shot down. I knew Bob from army flight school where we all lived together in the "zoo." The mission was very secret at the time because President Nixon was denying involvement across the border; but our guys were doing it (along with the army and air force in a combined mission out of Quang Tri).

Larry and the others were immediately declared KIA (unusual without bodies—except in this case). A bogus story was floated that they got lost and flew into Laos and were shot down. Larry did E&E for 19 days, and during that time he was "buried" by his family back home. Then he was rescued by an army Huey doing the same mission and was brought to Da Nang for medical treatment, debrief (me) and then evacuation to the USA.

He called his mom and announced he was actually alive. Then the heavies (senior command officers) demanded a debrief ASAP so he could go home. We spent a week recounting the incident. Then we signed a non-disclosure document and promised not to tell the story for five years. After it was realized that Larry survived, the concern was that someone else might be out there.

A team was put into the crash site (I saw the photos and read the debrief). They found footprints and a lot of molten metal—as if someone had dragged pieces away. The conclusion was that the other three crew members were killed in the crash (Bob did a good enough autorotation to allow Larry to survive—although Larry described a cockpit engulfed in flame). Some bones and dental work were recovered, but I don't know whom it was associated with.*

HML-167 continued supporting the southern portion of the Eagle Claw mission until late June. One of the last missions involved Lt Larry Grandy, Comprise 17. He described it this way:

I was scheduled to fly with a captain on an Eagle Claw, Mission 72, and it was my check ride to be an Eagle Claw mission commander. This was after the Marine Corps picked up the south part of the mission and it was flown completely by Marine aircraft out of Marble. We were flying a slick Huey.

We would fly to An Hoa for refueling and then go west across the "wire" for inserts/extracts, FOB resupply/medevac, etc. So Mike and I briefed with the Cobras from 367 and the '53 and '46 transports at Marble. It was an AM daytime mission with good weather all the way. Takeoff was normal. We were flying out to an FOB in Laos to pull out some medevacs that had been wounded by booby traps on a patrol. As we circled up over Cao Do bridge, I did a power check and determined that our engine was very, very sick, high temp and low torque. We flew the mission as advertised and were returning with the medevacs aboard one of the '53s.

---

* USMC/Vietnam Helicopter Association—KIA Database—NOTAM Board, Submission by Lt Paul Pratt.

On return, about ten miles east of the FOB, our sick engine went "BONK" and would not relight. The captain did the auto to a very thick bamboo thicket with a nice touchdown and no enemy in the area. The bamboo was so thick and compressed by the weight of the Huey that I could only touch the ground with one foot. Couldn't get the KYs (KY-28's an electronic device used to "scramble" the voice transmissions) out of their mounts, so Mike and I shot rounds into them to ruin their codes and capabilities.

We communicated with the Cobras and '53s that we were all OK and the '53 dropped the "Jacob's ladder" on top of our aircraft. We all boarded the ladder one at a time and we were transported, hanging under the '53 all the way to An Hoa, where we got off one at a time in reverse order. That was one hell of an interesting ride. Mike and I bought the '53 crew a case of Scotch.

Our aircraft was externaled (caried as a sling load under the aircraft) out by another '53 that afternoon, and I flew the post-maintenance flight on it about 30 days later after the engine was replaced.

To the best of my knowledge, that was the last Eagle Claw mission 167 flew. We were too slow and, frankly, unnecessary for the mission since it was now an all–Marine Corps operation. The Cobras led all the Eagle Claw missions after that.*

Rest in Peace
1stLt Robert E. Castle
SSgt Thomas H. Underwood
Sgt David Gonzales
March 21, 1970

---

* As related to the author by Lt Larry Grandy via email, January 26, 2024.

25

April Fools

Capping off March, I was assigned to take one of two gunships to Chu Lai for an overnight stay. I had just returned from Phu Bai where I was on standby with the Eagle Claw mission. I had been there from eight in the morning until 1730 (5:30 p.m.). I spent most of the day sitting around, only had one side trip out to LZ60A with three passengers and totaled about two and a half hours of flight time.

We had a mostly lazy day March 31, hanging around the squadron. The plan called for us to take the gunships to Chu Lai, leaving about 1800, then returning on April 1, arriving at Marble Mountain around 0730. On all my previous overnight missions, we had at least 12 hours off before flying again. This time, oh well, it was April 1!

The new plan, after arriving at Marble Mountain, is that I had been assigned another copilot. So I quickly changed aircraft (the copilot had already pre-flighted) and launched at 0810 for another overnight stay in Phu Bai, again standing by in a slick for an Eagle Claw mission. No problem. We would get back around 0600 on the 2nd, and then I could enjoy a day off! Right! Wrong! This April Fool's joke is continuing.

We shut down at 0610 and headed to the ready room to file our after-action report. There was nothing to report—flew about two hours, most of that in transit between Marble Mountain and Phu Bai. As soon as I finished the paperwork from the last flight, the operations duty officer said, "Grab a seat. You are briefing in a few minutes. You are the copilot in the second aircraft in a section of guns heading back to Phu Bai." The good news: I would be flying copilot with my good friend Lt Tom Broderick.

So much for no Marines north of the Hai Van Pass. I was starting to wonder if I should have my personal effects shipped to Phu Bai! The operations duty officer said, "No problem, you'll be back around six tonight."

We launched, sat around waiting for something to happen all day, nothing did and returned at 1810, when I found out that I would have the next morning off. I wouldn't have to launch until after lunch on the 3rd. Gosh, twelve hours off, half of which I would spend sleeping, walking to and from my quarters and finding something to eat. No wonder I didn't have time to write home.

The mission on the 3rd was to take a visiting colonel to half a dozen patrol sites between LZ Baldy and Liberty Bridge for command visits. That wrapped up at around 1800. Good thing I have some C rations in my quarters because the mess is definitely going to be closed before I could get there. Maybe I'll have the 4th off?

Nope! Got another early morning brief: flying in the right seat in the second aircraft in a section of guns. Section lead for this mission was my hooch mate Lt Jenks Jenkins, Comprise 21. The mission is armed escort for the Seventh Marine Regiment for areas around LZ Baldy. Hope they have plenty of smoke; their map-reading skills, more often than not, leave a little to be desired. We wrapped up this mission without contact and without difficulty with about six hours of flight time.

Many times during the year, I was assigned multiple missions but never back to back to back like this six-day period from the end of March through April 4. I did get three days off and did not have to fly again until April 8.

Overall, April was a little slower than previous months. I flew around the same number of missions, but most were a little shorter in length. Prior to the rescue of Lt Parsons, I flew a couple of Eagle Claw missions, some resupply escort and medevac escort, without much enemy activity, until the end of the month.

26

Sniffing Out the Enemy

Once Larry was picked up, we forced a restructure of the Eagle Claw mission. It would no longer be a multi-service mission. The transports would be Phrogs from one of our CH-46 squadrons, escorts would be Cobras from 367 and guns from 167. The package would include a CH-53 (to recover any downed aircraft) and a single slick Huey with a hoist to assist with the recovery of any surviving crew members.

I flew 16 gunship missions and 5 slick missions for only 63.2 hours this month. The gunship missions were a mixture of medevac, resupply and VR (APD) escort flights. On one of the VR escort missions, we were requested by DASC to engage some VC in the open. We were able to accomplish that with some well-placed rockets. We were carrying some fléchette rockets, and I was lucky enough to put a rocket between two VCs, pinning one of them to a tree and removing the other from any further combat action.

Occasionally, our friends weren't very friendly! On a gunship escort for a night medevac mission on April 11–12, I was flying wing on Capt RT. We launched about 1800 over to the medevac standby hut. During the night, we were called out four times for emergency medevacs. On the second callout of the night, we received fire from an ARVN compound about 2,000 meters south of the medevac location. We rated the fire as between moderate and intense. The fire was confirmed by U.S. observers located on Hill 327. I noted on the after-action report that some of the tracers appeared to be close enough to touch. Since the fire was confirmed as coming from the "friendly" compound, we did not return the compliment.

One of the more routine missions we were assigned was called APD. It was sometimes called detection of concealed personnel (DCP). It required a low-flying aircraft to take samples of air over the jungle through a large hose similar to a clothes dryer vent hose that was attached to the air vent in the copilot's chin bubble, then routed under the copilot's seat and fed into a machine in the back of the aircraft. The machine would analyze the air sample for concentrations of nitrogen and ammonia, which were given off by large amounts of urine, usually present because of a concentration of troops in the field.

The system came with an operator, who called out the readings so we all knew when we were flying over a troop encampment. We normally flew this mission with two pilots and the "sniffer" operator and without a crew chief. We called it the sniffer mission. The sniffer mission is routine until it isn't.

The mission requirements called for a section of gunships to follow the "sniffer" aircraft to provide immediate air support and an ability to call in additional support whenever and wherever bad guys were found. Occasionally, there was also an OV-10 (fixed-wing, turbo-prop aircraft with a pilot and an aerial observer for crew) assigned to trail us around. The aerial observer was an expert in "call for fire" and was extremely valuable when (not if) you got in trouble. The OV-10 also was capable of carrying a few 2.75-inch rockets with white phosphorous warheads to serve as spotting rounds for fixed-wing air to provide ground support. In other mission roles, the OV-10 could also carry four recon Marines in a cramped compartment behind the pilot for deep insertion by parachute. The Marines in the back would bail out when over the insertion point.

An airborne personnel detection mission heading out.

26. Sniffing Out the Enemy

The flight lead for the mission on April 28 was "Marvelous Marv" and his crew; I was flying aircraft commander in dash two. For the two lieutenants in the low bird, it turned out to be a long day. Actually, for all of us, it was a long eventful day.

We flew this particular day's mission in a slightly mountainous region west southwest of Da Nang. The Hueys we flew were not overpowered, especially at altitude. One of the things we learned early on was not to get the aircraft in situations where lots of power would be required to get out of a bad spot. If you had to fly low and slow (we did for this mission), you never flew "up" a draw. The sides get steep, and the draw gets narrow. Power required can easily exceed power available.

For the first half hour of this flight, all we heard on the radio was the quiet report of the "sniffer" operator saying "no contact" or "low contact." Low contact was usually a small group of jungle animals.

As we got into the second half hour, we started hearing "strong reading—possible contact," then "very strong reading—probable contact." As the low bird pursued this contact, we noticed that the pilot was starting to fly up a draw at low altitude.

As the operator reported his highest reading for the entire mission, the pilot recognized his position and attempted to turn around. Unfortunately, he ran out of airspeed, altitude and ideas all at the same time. The aircraft impacted the west wall of the valley, split into two pieces, with the cockpit sliding down one side of the mountain wall and the cabin down the other. The fuel cell for a Huey is under the floor of the cabin, and with the impact, the cabin, cockpit, and tail section burst into flame. Shortly after impact, we heard the mayday call from the pilot using his handheld emergency radio. "Marv" had notified Da Nang DASC of the situation and a rescue effort was immediately underway. All aircraft with unexpended ordnance were told to contact "Marv" on our working frequency and a pair of "Jolly Green Giants," U.S. Air Force rescue helicopters, were launched from Da Nang AFB.

Within minutes, we had sections of A-4s, F-4s and Spads (ARVN A-1Es) checking in. As we approached the site, we began taking small-arms fire from the area of the last strong reading. Marv vectored the attack and fighter aircraft with the least fuel remaining into the site first. The OV-10 provided marking rounds for the fixed-wing bombing runs. The Spads had five hours of fuel, 250- and 500-pound bombs, 30-caliber machine guns and smoke available. For information, an A-1E is a single-engine, prop-driven, single-pilot, post–World War II–era ground attack aircraft.

At Marv's direction, the A-4s and F-4s began expending their ordnance on target. Once "Winchester" (out of ordnance), the A-4s and

F-4s went RTB (return to base). The Jolly Greens attempted their first approach but had to wave off due to intense small-arms fire from the region. Marv and I made several gun and rocket runs into the area between fixed-wing ordnance drops. Then Marv called in the Spads.

They set up parallel runs dropping most of their ordnance, then circled back around and laid down smoke around the rescue site. The winds over the mountain blew the rising smoke over so that a tunnel was formed, and the Jolly Greens flew inside the tunnel to make the hoist pickup. They hovered in place for a while and were able to pick up the pilot and copilot. They were evacuated to "Charlie Med" and earned a trip back to the States.

At some point in the middle of this rescue, Marv and I returned to Marble Mountain to refuel and rearm. The total mission time was about three and a half hours.

As we got the enemy fire under control, the Mission 80 rapid reaction crew (two Phrogs with a platoon of Marines and two gunships) were launched from Marble Mountain and inserted on the other side of the hill where the cabin slid down. Unfortunately, the "sniffer" operator, initially reported as missing in action, was killed, but we were able to recover his body to be returned to his family. Both pilots suffered some burns and were medevaced for treatment.

The OV-10 remained on station, prepared to call in artillery as soon as the rescues and body recoveries were complete. This "simple" mission would claim more bodies before we got out of Vietnam.

Rest in Peace
Cpl David C. Bugman
APD Operator
April 28, 1970

27

Rockets Across the Demilitarized Zone

By mid–February, all the Marine aviation assets had moved from Phu Bai to Marble Mountain, although we still supported some limited operations in the northern area of I corps. The army was responsible for most operations in that area, which were supported by their vast collection of Hueys. Their Hueys also did most of their resupply. In 1970, they had only Chinooks (CH-47), which were heavy-lift aircraft, and Hueys. They did not have any medium-lift aircraft similar to our Phrogs. For all resupply missions in the later months, we provided a section of guns as escort. Although for normal resupply, enemy contact was not expected, we didn't take any chances. Emergency resupply was usually just ammunition and water; that normally occurred when a unit was in contact with the enemy, and in that case, we went in guns blazing.

The ARVN also operated extensively in that area and was supported by their own H-34s. We were occasionally called to support them with guns as well.

Today's mission was just that: escort some resupply Phrogs into the area north of Phu Bai to resupply several ARVN outposts. The supplies were to be staged at Phu Bai; refueling and additional ordnance, if needed, would also be there. Anytime we worked in the north, it was going to be a long day, starting with the briefing, then pre-flight, flight to get there, work with whoever for a while, refuel when necessary, the flight home, post-flight and finally write the after-action report. The job is not complete until the paperwork is done.

The only thing this mission lacked was enemy contact. We resupplied half a dozen outposts with no contact. The blades on our Hueys had a long chord (distance from the leading edge of the blade to the trailing edge), so when we pulled off a gun run, we truly beat the air into submission. The noise alone should scare the VC/NVA into keeping their heads down. It must have worked today; after several hours of making simulated gun runs while the Phrogs delivered rations, ammunition and water to the ARVN, we had not fired a single rocket or bullet.

After the last unit had been served, the Phrogs headed to Phu Bai to top off their tanks and then back to Marble Mountain. We were still near the demilitarized zone (DMZ) with a full load of rockets and bullets. Gosh, we can't go home with all this ordnance! The solution: we cleared it with the northernmost outpost and made a gun run toward the DMZ. As we got very close to the border of the DMZ, we pulled the nose up about 15 degrees and fired all our rockets in salvo; seven pairs launched sequentially! The propellant in the rockets sent them soaring; not sure how far they went or if they ever hit anything besides the ground, but I had launched my personal strike against North Vietnam and the Communist Party. Also, I never heard any repercussions about this event.

28

Magnet Ass

After April, there were no more slow months. In May, I flew almost 94 hours; in June, 89 hours; in July, 88 hours; in August, 87 hours.

Most times, the nickname we got in our first unit stuck with us for our entire career, whether 3 years or 25 years. Every once in a while, an extraordinary event would cause that to change. This is one such happening.

The mission was simple: pick up a general and his strap hangers at Da Nang AFB and drop them at Chu Lai AFB, a flight of about 45 minutes due south of Da Nang. The aircraft was prepped and VIPed (it had some fancy red seat cushions and seat belt covers installed and the oil and grease spills were wiped up).

My crew chief and I briefed, pre-flighted and headed to Da Nang for our pickup. The VIPs were on time, the weather was clear and dry and the flight to Chu Lai was uneventful. After dropping off the VIPs, we refueled, double-checked the weather and headed back.

On the return trip, the crew chief was riding in the left (copilot's) seat, and I let him fly a little (we did this every chance we could; never knew when the crew chief might have to fly the aircraft—you know, enemy fire and that sort of thing). Hal Walker describes just such an event in an HMM-364 Phrog when the pilot was killed and the copilot wounded by the same bullet. When that happened, the crew chief locked the pilot in place with his harness lock, sat in his lap and flew the Phrog back to the medevac pad. The copilot only assisted with the landing.*

We chose to fly back at 3,500 feet, well out of small-arms range. There were no known anti-aircraft missiles in South Vietnam; the only time we worried about that was if we went north—way north or sometimes west. At that altitude, we could almost see our destination.

We were cruising along, fat, dumb and happy. Had a slight tailwind;

---

* Walker, Harold G., *The Grotto*, Book Two, Dragonfly Publishing, 182–197.

it was smooth sailing, just the kind of day when nothing could go wrong, right?

Harry Reasoner had a few comments about helicopter pilots being brooding, worrying introverts; if nothing was wrong, we should be expecting something to go wrong. For a news guy, he was pretty prophetic.

As we flew along, we heard a loud smack. The crew chief and I looked at each other with a "what the hell?" expression. We both knew the sound—the sound of a bullet hitting metal. At 3,500 feet? Crap, are you kidding me? Now what? This was not the first time I had been shot at and wouldn't be the last, but this rifleman had to be the luckiest shot in the world!

I took over the controls of the aircraft and didn't notice anything significantly different. The gauges were all normal; there were no warning or caution lights, no fire warning. I made port and starboard turns, adjusted the pitch of the rotor blades. Nothing—the controls were all normal, the aircraft responded to control changes, the engine was normal, the rotor speed was exactly where it was supposed to be. We didn't appear to be losing fuel, oil or hydraulic fluid. So what next?

I reported to Da Nang DASC that I had received small-arms fire, the aircraft had been hit but appeared normal and that we were proceeding to Marble Mountain Airfield. I called the squadron on the base FM radio and reported the same. I was instructed to proceed to base, not to refuel and that we would be met on the flight line.

As we taxied in, I could see that the AMO, the assistant AMO, the flight line officer, quality assurance inspector and a large number of maintenance workers were waiting for us to park and shut down. As soon as the rotors were stopped and tied down, they all descended on the aircraft, I just stood out of the way and watched. The aircraft was searched with a fine-tooth comb, but nothing stood out. Finally, one of the maintenance crew climbed out from under the aircraft, opened the pilot's door and looked under the armor-plated seat. (Remember me talking about testing the quality of the armor-plating protection theory?) After a couple of minutes, he went to the AMO, then both came to me. The maintenance man held out his hand and offered me a piece of crumpled lead that he had scraped off the bottom of the seat.

For those in the know, I was now known as "Magnet Ass." You might think this story ends here, but no—years later, I told this story to my kindergarten-age son.

A few weeks later, his mother was approached by his teacher, who was desperately trying to keep a straight face. She wanted to know how I had become known as "Maggot Ass." Remember, everything you tell a child *will* be repeated, just not necessarily verbatim!

29

Reviewing the Troops

May was the busiest month I had in Vietnam. A short, armed escort for resupply early on the 1st, followed by a Chu Lai fly-away for the night and then another armed escort resupply on the 2nd. Medevac escort and a longish VIP flight for division followed.

The commanding general of the First Marine Division (1stMarDiv), MGen C.F. Widdecke tasked a mission so he could review the troops and have some firsthand meetings with his regimental and battalion commanders. I was assigned the mission; this was not the first time I had flown this sort of a mission, nor would it be the last. Earlier in the year, I had flown LtGen Nickerson, III MAF commanding general, around for one of his last visits before being relieved by LtGen McCutcheon. This time, I was being "chased" by Lt Hal Walker, Chatterbox 28, in his Phrog. The last time I was chased by another Chatterbox aircraft and Hal was the copilot, we got shot at. I hoped that history did not repeat itself. I liked to keep everything quiet and smooth when carrying general officers.

MGen Widdecke and his sergeant major asked to be taken to each of the regimental headquarters and as many of the battalion headquarters as we could work in. Hal Walker, Chatterbox 28, was chasing us on his seventh flight as aircraft commander. His role was to follow me wherever the general wanted to go and pick us up if there was trouble. I hoped he was bored out of his mind. Hal related that he was well entertained by his copilot on this six-and-a-half-hour journey.*

Getting promoted to the flag officer ranks (brigadier general, major general, lieutenant general and general) was an advancement that required competence as well as some political glad-handing, and MGen Widdecke was no exception. He was lean and rugged and exemplified everything you expect of a general officer. He could

---

* Walker, Harold G., *The Grotto*, Book Two, Dragonfly Publishing, 249–250.

correct your mistakes, give you new direction and make you feel good about it.

I met Hal and his crew at LZ400, the division headquarters landing zone, and briefed what I knew about today's mission. We decided that we would play it by ear, keeping each other informed about our fuel status and expected wait times at our various stops. When the general and his party came aboard the aircraft, I informed Hal our first stop would be the airfield at An Hoa; we could top our fuel tanks as soon as the general headed off to his first meeting.

All generals in positions of command have an aide assigned (truly a thankless position). So as soon as I could, I touched base with the aide and requested that when the general is about to leave each of his meetings that the aide send us notification. That way, we could have the aircraft started and ready to depart; the general would not have to wait on us. After leaving LZ400, we continued south on the west side of Da Nang AFB, intercepted the red line (Highway 1) south of Marble Mountain, continued south to the river, then west to An Hoa. We dropped the general and his party at the airfield, repositioned to the fuel pits, then after all the tanks had been topped off, moved to the parking area

An Hoa Airfield, Southern I Corps, RVN.

29. Reviewing the Troops

and shut down, waiting for the general's return. While we were parked there, I talked to Hal and his crew for a bit. Conversation was a little difficult because the eight-inch guns just off the end of the runway were conducting a fire mission into the Arizona area, a known hangout for VC and NVA forces.

After about 45 minutes we got the word that the general was wrapping up his meeting and would be ready to depart within ten minutes. Hal and I got our aircraft started, and as soon as the general was aboard, he said he wanted to swing north into the Arizona for a quick look-see before we headed over to Baldy. Leaving An Hoa, we checked in with DASC for clearance, got a look at what the big guns had been shooting, then headed over to Baldy. The An Hoa sequence was repeated at Baldy, then over to Hill 55.

When the general had finished his visits, we returned him to LZ400. Then Hal and I headed back to Marble Mountain. Hal told me that he and his crew had been listening to Armed Forces Radio; they were having a Beatles marathon with several repeated renditions of "Hey, Jude." I wasn't so fortunate since the general and his aide both had on headsets and were able to monitor everything said in the aircraft.

30

Hogs and Napalm

The CH-53s were introduced in Vietnam to replace the aging H-34s, which were the workhorse of the Marines. Unfortunately, their missions were restricted. In 1969 dollars, they were the most expensive helicopter the Marine Corps owned, and nobody wanted to lose one of them. They primarily hauled supplies from major facility to major facility and were used to recover downed aircraft, while the CH-46s carried the load in the field (and suffered significant losses).

During its operational test phase, acrobatic flight consisting of a loop and a roll were demonstrated by Marine test pilot LtCol Bob Guay. There are many films around showing these maneuvers. In early 1970, LtCol Guay was assigned to MAG 16 as the operations officer, and he led the charge to get the Hogs into the fight.

The 53s were a twin-engine aircraft capable of sustained flight on a single engine. Their six-bladed rotor system had enough lead and lax (forward and aft movement of each individual blade) to allow it to lose a rotor blade and continue flight for a short time. The twin hydraulic systems were isolated from each other without action from the pilots and each were sufficient to allow full control of the aircraft. Although full employment posed some risks, its speed and maneuverability were significant assets. The air force was already using a heavily armored version known as the Jolly Green Giant for emergency recovery of downed pilots. They even gave out certificates to pilots they had recovered.*

Soon, the governing powers relented; the 53s could participate. Their mission role was expanded to include large troop inserts, extracts and resupply of units in the field, but because of their size (the free world's largest helicopter), they were not a good fit for the medevac role.

The Marine Corps (especially Marines in combat) is always looking for ways to expand their role, probably from a legitimate fear of being

---

* Walker, Harold G., *The Grotto*, Book Two, Dragonfly Publishing, 447.

30. Hogs and Napalm

absorbed into the army (ground forces) and the navy (aviation assets). We knew that napalm was very effective against the extensive tunnel system that the VC and NVA were using against us, if only there were a way to get more of it into play. Currently, only ground attack jets were delivering it, and although the explosions and subsequent fire were spectacular, there had to be a way to get more of it into the soil and the tunnels.

The plan—have a section of 53s carry about twenty 55-gallon drums of napalm in a cargo net, drop it from altitude about 1,000–1,500 feet above ground level (AGL). The barrels would burst, allow the napalm to soak in the tunnel complex for a few minutes, then ignite it with a white phosphorus (also known as Willie Pete) warhead and high explosives from a rocket fired by one of our gunships.

The first such mission was executed on May 8, against an extensive enemy underground complex consisting of both hardened bunkers and a hospital complex that had been identified in the Que Son mountains. When dropped, the barrels burst open, allowing 1,100 gallons of deadly napalm to filter into the underground complex. After just a few minutes, the guns rolled in hot. High explosives rained along the axis of the napalm and ignited a giant fire. Battle damage assessment by a recon team inserted later showed 200 VC/NVA killed in the underground fire.*

---

* Walker, Harold G., *The Grotto*, Book Two, Dragonfly Publishing, 243–244.

31

Crew Rest

It seemed liked forever. We got four trips out of country; the first was to the Philippines for JEST (three or four days there with most of one day actually spent training). I had barely gotten used to being in Vietnam when that trip occurred. R&R in Australia was soon after (late in my third month). Then leave in Taipei came in mid–March. I did a lot of drinking and some sightseeing there. Now the fourth and final trip: crew rest—four days in Udorn, Thailand.

No more fancy Boeing 707s for the wicked; we were traveling on the old workhorse, the C-117, a slightly modernized and militarized version of the DC-3. We still had to get to Da Nang to board, but since there were several of us going, the squadron hauled us over in a truck. There were three of us from 167 and a few others from other squadrons. Departure was mid-afternoon, and it would be getting late when we arrived. We would have to fly over some bad-guy country to get there. So leaving Vietnam, the aircraft would climb out to the east until reaching a safe altitude, then turn west, crossing Laos and into Thailand.

Arriving there, we were transported to the hotel and told when to be back. That was the last semblance of military supervision. Near the hotel, we could exchange MPC for American green or write checks for cash at an American bank. At the hotel, we got individual rooms and were met in the lobby by a "tailor" who fitted us for whatever style and quantity clothing we wanted. He promised it would be ready the night before we departed. I ordered a couple of sport coats, a couple of suits and some shirts. The total cost—about $200.

Just off the lobby was a barber shop where you could get a haircut, shave and a massage. I got the haircut, shave and a brief neck message. I really didn't like the shave with the straight razor and have never gotten one since.

My friend "Lonesome George" had told me about the "Holiday Inn" not far from our hotel; he said I really had to visit there. At the time,

31. Crew Rest

I didn't understand what could be so interesting about an American motel chain. But following his advice, I went there the next day with Injun Joe. As we got to the front of the building, there was the giant green bent arrow with "Holiday Inn" spelled out, just like in the States.

That was where the resemblance ended. We walked in the front door and noted that the left wall was all glass with three elevated rows of seating behind it. Scattered through the seating were many young, beautiful girls in white lab coats. Each girl had a number in front of her chair. This "Holiday Inn" was a giant massage parlor. When checking in, you gave the clerk a number, and the lady with that number was your massage therapist for the next couple of hours. Each massage came with a steam bath, cold cleansing shower and a full body massage. This place was going to be the perfect recovery site after a full night of drinking. For a very nominal fee, the ladies would leave with you and provide guide/translator services for you while you shopped.

Injun Joe and I took advantage of the opportunity to see some of the smaller shops in Udorn and look for some bargains. Thailand is known for its black star sapphires, and I was able purchase a ring for my little finger set with a black star sapphire in 24-carat gold between two small topaz chips. Topaz is my birthstone. The jeweler promised to have it ready the morning we were to depart; I would have to get up in time

(From left) Lt Hugenberg, (unidentified), Fleener, Lt Hall and Lt Heiberg returning from crew rest in Udorn.

to be at his store by 5:30 a.m. That was a significant challenge since we were spending so much time drinking, but I made it.

We did spend a little time sitting by the pool and relaxing, but most of our spare time was spent shopping and drinking. I did find time to go to the bank and send a check to my brother for his upcoming wedding.

Our flight home was the same as our flight here, just in reverse and with a little more luggage to carry.

32

Meritorious Copilot

The seven days after Udorn were very busy—all long days, mostly armed escort for resupply, medevac, VR, and APD. On the 19th, I stepped in it and didn't come out smelling like a rose.

You've heard the expression "letting your alligator mouth overload your hummingbird ass"? Sometimes your desire to accomplish a mission gets you into that kind of situation. Unfortunately, flying in combat doesn't really allow that because you take so many others with you! This is a tale with a price where I got in deeper than my experience level allowed, and unfortunately, it cost me a little and put others at significant risk.

We had several missions each day which were always assigned. They were generally flown single pilot with a crew chief in a slick aircraft. LtGen McCutcheon, commanding general, III MAF, and BGen Miller (father of the AV-8), chief of staff, III MAF, each got a single VIPed Huey every day. One Huey and one Phrog (CH-46) were assigned each day to the Korean unit and to the Fifth and Seventh Marine Regiments, respectively. Also, a Phrog and a Huey were assigned to the commanding generals of First Marine Division and First Marine Air Wing.

This mission was with the Fifth Marines, working out of An Hoa airfield. When the Marines were in the field, they carried lots of smoke so we could find them; their map-reading skills left a little to be desired.

A few days before this mission, the powers that be decreed that we could only have a maximum of five people on our Hueys including crew (this was later rescinded but not in time to protect my sorry ass). Some desk jockey thought it was too hot to carry the weight of more than five people. It really wasn't; you just had to manage your fuel load and the situations that you got into!

We were just coming out of the monsoon season, and as the rains died out, all the rivers and streams were super swollen. The day before this mission, a couple of Marines from the Fifth Marines had fallen off a bridge and drowned. Their bodies had not been recovered, and our job was to recon the river from An Hoa for a few miles downstream to see if they could be found.

Anyway, on this mission the regimental ops officer rode in the copilot's seat, while we searched the river for any sign of the bodies. About eight miles downstream from where the Marines had fallen, there was a collapsed railroad bridge partially settled in the river. As we went by the bridge, my crew chief reported seeing some clothing and possibly a body entangled in the bridge wreckage. After a couple of low passes, we were able to confirm that there was indeed a body trapped in the wreckage. We were able to identify an area nearby where a squad could be inserted. They would then move to the bridge to attempt the recovery.

What should have happened is, I report the discovery to DASC; they launch Mission 80 with two Phrogs, two gunships and a squad of Marines to recover the body. Instead, I undertook the mission with the assets already assigned.

Returning to An Hoa, we topped off the fuel tanks, briefed the Phrog chase crew and loaded up. The Phrog took a squad of Marines, and I added a ground radio operator and two Marines to provide fire support out the doors of the aircraft, with the operations officer acting as an observer. Anybody with reasonable math skills now knows that we have six people on the Huey. Not a flight problem but over the artificially imposed limit.

Back at the bridge, I made a low pass to confirm that the body was still in the wreckage—it was—then spotted the landing zone for the Phrog. The '46 hit the zone, offloaded the squad and resumed circling at altitude. I made a couple of low passes, flying over the Marines working their way toward the bridge so they had a visual reference for the route to the bridge. The jungle had overgrown the area; their travels were slow and methodical, but they were making good progress en route to the bridge.

As the troops reached the bridge, I extended my low pass slightly to the north and flew over a small field of old, rusty oil drums. When I went by the barrels, a VC soldier stood up and fired off a series of shots toward our aircraft. I heard the rounds impacting the aircraft, and my crew chief reported that he was wounded as well as the ground radio operator and one of the Marine riflemen. When the VC get lucky, they get really lucky.

I immediately gained altitude, radioed the Phrog that we had been hit, had wounded aboard and were headed for "Charlie Med" back at Da Nang. As we flew back, about a 20-minute trip, I radioed Da Nang DASC, reported the incident, asked for a rapid response crew to launch

32. Meritorious Copilot

to the site to support the troops on the ground and explained the medical situation on my aircraft. The Phrog followed me back to "Charlie Med," and I was met by several corpsmen with stretchers to offload the wounded. The aircraft didn't seem to have any critical damage, so I returned to base with the Ops O and everybody else who wasn't wounded.

At Marble Mountain, my commanding officer informed me that there had been a recent report of enemy activity in that area that I had failed to catch at the morning intel briefing and then reminded me of the five-man limit. As a result, he restricted me to flying as a copilot until he said different and preferred that I only fly with an experienced company grade officer or field grade officer during that period.

Later that night, he took me to "Charlie Med" in his jeep to visit with my crew chief. He was out of surgery and a little out of it but in pretty good spirits. His wound, though not minor, was not life threatening, and he was getting a free ticket back to the States. The others were also out of danger and were heading home.

"Charlie Med" landing pad for the naval hospital in Da Nang.

With this incident, I learned a valuable lesson: fly the aircraft, pay attention to the briefings, know the rules and follow them. Sometimes even when you screw up, all ends fairly well! The wounds were all minor, just enough to earn a ride home and I was getting a well-deserved but minor disciplinary action.

I had the 20th off. Then from the 21st to the 30th, I flew a lot of hours on a variety of missions, mostly gunship escort for the usual missions. On the 31st, I was the copilot for the low bird on a VR of the Rocket Belt around Da Nang.

33

Troop Insert

Beginning my purgatory as "meritorious copilot," I was assigned to fly with Capt "Marvelous Marv" for this flight—another good guy and good pilot on his second tour in Vietnam. We were escorting a division (four aircraft) of "Hogs" (CH-53s) doing a massive troop insert into the Arizona area near the An Hoa valley in the southern I Corps area of South Vietnam.

Historically, the Arizona was infamous for VC and NVA activity. Intel said the area of the insert had recently had some moderate enemy activity, and the regiment was going to sweep the area to clean out any pockets of resistance.

U.S. policy for this war had abandoned the capture-and-hold territory policy of World War II in favor of sweeping through an area, denying its use to an enemy, then returning to a fixed position—expecting the populace to hold its own territory. (This didn't work as we were constantly fighting the same battles through the same territory. Apparently, the word was not getting back to the powers making the decisions because the policy never changed.)

We briefed early, then met the CH-53 crews at the regimental headquarters at LZ Baldy and briefed the mission with them. Our flight of two Huey gunships would proceed the '53s into the insert area and conduct a quick aerial reconnaissance. Then, as the first flight of Hogs approached, we would randomly fire rockets and M-60 machine guns through the area, unless a specific target revealed itself. After the first load of troops was dropped off, we would refuel and rearm while the '53s got another load of troops. This sequence would be repeated several times throughout the expected five- to six-hour mission. Once all the troops were on the ground, we would be on call to react to any enemy activity encountered by the ground guys. A couple of days later, a mission would be put together to extract the forces that we had inserted.

In the Huey (as well as in the '53s), there is a foot switch, similar to the old headlight dimmer switch in cars, that would allow the pilot not flying to transmit on either the radio or intercom as appropriate. The pilot flying the aircraft would normally use the trigger switch on the cyclic to transmit (the cyclic trigger is a two-position switch: the first indent, the pilot would transmit on the intercom; the second indent activated whichever radio was active). Another option was to select "Hot Mic," then adjust the "Vox" so you were not continuously broadcasting. With the "Vox" properly adjusted, the microphone would only transmit when you started talking. I used this procedure often, especially in later years when I was instructing.

As "flight lead," Capt Marv maintained control of the aircraft, flying, talking and shooting. An additional push button located on the top left of the cyclic fired either the rockets or guns, depending on which was armed (there is a separate arming panel where the pilot or copilot can select rockets—singles, pairs, or salvo or guns). My only task was to switch the Arm/Safe switch on the armament panel, select rockets or guns as directed and retune the radio to whichever frequency that was required whenever the pilot commanded it.

It was another bright, sunshiny day, with clear skies. The first recon and insert went off without incident as we raced through the area. After about an hour in the area, we pulled off and flew to An Hoa airstrip to refuel and rearm. There was plenty of room in the fuel pits for both our aircraft, but the rearming area was a little tighter, so on most missions we continued the procedure of one of us refueling while the other rearmed. Once complete, we switched positions.

Usually while rearming, one of the pilots would get out, stretch his legs and answer the call of nature, then relieve the other pilot so he could do the same. As it turned out, this was the only time today I touched the flight controls—while Marvelous Marv was relieving himself.

Back in the drop zone, we repeated what we had done before, escorting the '53s into and out of the area, spraying bullets and rockets randomly outside the perimeter of the sweep area where the troops were working. As the Hogs headed back to get more troops, we lingered to make sure we weren't needed to respond to any enemy activity, then headed back to refuel and rearm again. We repeated this sequence several times.

As you will see in "Rocket Training," I harbor a little inner "wise-ass." After three times of this sequence, I let it sneak out! We were on our fourth run, with Marvelous Marv still flying, talking and shooting. I dropped the window (in the Huey, the pilot's side windows slide up and down and were held in place with a friction knob) on my side of

33. Troop Insert

the aircraft, took out my .38 and fired off a round into the wilderness. This was the only time in my year in Vietnam that I fired my personal weapon (now I was going to have to clean it).

The explosion of the .38 round scared the crap out of Marvelous Marv, and I got a well-deserved ass-chewing for my action, but I figure it was worth it. At least I got to shoot once. Not sure if Marvelous Marv ever figured out why I did it. It still made a great story among the LPA at the club.

34

A Flight Demonstration

In the early days of October through December 1969, we had trouble with the availability of aircraft to support the missions we were assigned; we were well below our Table of Organization (T/O), and the Marines we had aboard were doing double duty. (A Table of Organization is a HQMC-generated document that specifies how many Marines and what Military Occupation Specialty [MOS] each squadron is supposed to have to operate efficiently. A T/O is usually based on a 12-airplane squadron and we were growing into a 45-aircraft unit.) Every aircraft launched had to have a crew chief, and every gunship had to have a crew chief and a gunner. The crew chiefs had a maintenance MOS; being a crew chief was an additional duty—they got extra money for flying, but that doesn't increase the number of maintainers available each day to fix and launch aircraft.

Gunners also got a stipend for agreeing to risk their lives as airborne operators of the M-60s on our gunships, but being a gunner was also an additional duty. While the gunners could be maintenance personnel, some of them came from other backgrounds—admin clerks, ops clerks, supply, and so on—but the majority were maintenance people. This meant that most of the maintenance done on aircraft was done at night, after flight operations secured.

In late December, we got aircraft from HML-367 as they transitioned from Hueys to Cobras. We also got some additional people, so availability gradually improved. We still didn't have enough, but things were getting better. Over the months of early spring, we got additional Marines from the States. We were now operating 42 aircraft with 6 being held in reserve. We had priority for parts, so that looked better as well, plus we could "borrow" parts from the reserve and crashed aircraft. We were flying between 2,000 and 3,000 hours per month as we moved into summer.

On May 17, HML-367 staged a flyover with 100 percent of their

34. A Flight Demonstration

Some "damaged" aircraft where we could occasionally get a few spare parts.

20-some aircraft. It was impressive; the sky was dark with aircraft. Not to be outdone (everybody knows that Marines are competitive, even [especially] among ourselves), we went to work. Maintenance was being done 24 hours a day; there was no letup. The 367 flyover could not stand alone in the annals of Marine history in Vietnam.

A "dimmer" CH-53 returning one of our aircraft.

May 31 was the day. Thirty-three gunships and slicks hit the sky over Marble Mountain. That was not a 100 percent flyover. Remember a couple of paragraphs ago I said we had 46 flyable aircraft. But between late January and May, we had crashed several; today, we had 34 flying, but 1 was conducting a mission. This Marine Corps flyover would stand for a while. In 1979, MAG-26 staged a 56-plane flyover, consisting of 25 CH-46s, 25 CH-53s, 2 Hueys and 4 Cobras. That one took the effort of three CH-46 squadrons (one composite doing workups for a "med" cruise) and two CH-53 squadrons.

35

Rocket Practice

All our captains were on their second tour in Vietnam. They were well respected, good pilots (they had survived a tour in Vietnam) and good guys. Most of the majors also were on their second tour. However, how well they were respected is another story. Most of the suspect ones had rotated out of country and the ones left behind weren't bad; in fact, I overnighted in Miami with our new XO as I was returning from my honeymoon a few years later.

Today, I was a copilot; my pilot was a captain, known by his initials "RT." Our launch today was an escort mission for some Phrogs running a resupply to a couple of ground units in the field. They were always in need of water, food and ammunition, usually in that order. Many times, the supplies were delivered via external lift, depending on the nature of the zone. If there was an area to land, the supplies were carried internally, and the Phrogs would land and offload. Today, we were going to an area with a large enough zone, so the Phrogs could land and deliver supplies. If the ground unit had been in recent contact with the enemy, the order of requirements usually changed to ammunition and water, and we didn't spend much time in the zone with deliveries.

Today, however, was routine, clear sky, warm weather, absolutely no enemy contact, so we spent lots of time circling, talking and observing the area around us, constantly vigilant against any threat.

Once all the resupplies were complete, the Phrogs headed back to base, and we got permission to expend some rockets and bullets for a little air-to-ground gunnery practice. It is not easy to shoot rockets in a Huey; the aiming system consisted of a painted cross on the windscreen and a fold-down sight in front of the pilot and copilot stations. On the end of the fold-down sight was a metal circle with two pieces of safety wire bisecting it up and down and left and right. The safety wire usually showed signs of adjustment (bending) by a previous pilot. The trick to shooting rockets was to line up the fold-down sight with the cross on the windscreen while in a moderate power on dive (10–12 degrees nose down) and the ball centered (aircraft in balanced flight), with your fingers crossed hoping that your rocket would strike somewhere in the correct grid square (1,000 meters on each side). The folding fins on our rockets didn't always deploy properly, and if that happened, the rocket would spin off-track faster than a politician's promise.

We found an abandoned bunker where there was no reported activity and got permission to use it as a target. RT was a pretty good shot and, after re-explaining the elements of rocket fire, placed all seven of the rockets in the right-hand pod within five to seven meters of the target bunker. After setting the armament system to safe and pulling off the target, he handed the aircraft to me and once again reviewed the shooting procedures.

I rolled in "hot" (armament system armed) and I fired my first rocket. It struck about five meters in front of the bunker. The second rocket went through the front opening of the bunker and blew out the back wall. Realizing that I was never going to repeat that performance, I enabled my inner wiseass, put the armament system on safe, pulled off the target and said, "Captain, do you want to take the rest of my pod and practice?" Probably not the best way to endear yourself to a senior officer!

RT was a pretty cool officer, so he didn't react to my comment; he just took control of the aircraft and acknowledged my extreme luck with the first pair of rockets. Afterward, we shared a few laughs with other

A comprise Huey firing a rocket.

35. Rocket Practice

pilots at the officers' club. Sometimes I got really lucky, both with my shooting and whoever was the brunt of my wiseass comments.

I didn't know it then, but this was my last flight on restriction. On June 5, I was the PQM on the low bird for the morning and afternoon Rocket Belt VR, then on the 6th, I had two more flights on the Rocket Belt VR, this time as the copilot on the gunship escort. On the 9th, I had Mission 7 in support of the ROK Marines single pilot. Then on the 10th, I was copilot on the lead gun for a night medevac escort.

36

Night Medevac
June 10 and 11, 1970

The blaring radio cut through a fitful sleep: "Marble Medevac, this is Da Nang DASC. I have an emergency medevac."

The radio call startled us from the drowsiness that masquerades as sleep. The other copilots and I and the crew chiefs and gunners began the sprint to the helicopter gunships and transports that sat quietly on the medevac standby pad, while the pilots listened to the details of the call. What was a quiet night in early 1970 was about to get exciting!

The use of medical evacuation helicopters in the Vietnam War had greatly reduced the fatalities incurred during combat operations by cutting the time between injury and hospitalization significantly. Knowing that time was important, the plan was to get the gunships out ahead of the Phrogs, allowing us to get to the medevac site ahead of the Phrogs so we could neutralize any enemy action before their arrival. Additionally, the Phrogs were faster in the air (but slower getting started) than the Hueys, so we needed to launch early. The copilots would get the aircraft started and ready to go while the aircraft commanders got the detailed brief.

First, some definitions. Medevacs are defined by their severity, the worst being "emergency," then "priority," followed by "routine" and then "permanent routine." An "emergency" medevac needs immediate high-level medical treatment to survive. A "priority" medevac can have treatment postponed for several hours. A "routine" medevac needs minor medical attention. A "permanent routine" is going home in a flag-draped box. During daylight hours, we launched for all categories of medevacs, but at night we only launched for priority and emergency medevacs. We only went into "hot" zones for "emergencies." A "hot" zone is an area that is actively involved in enemy contact and receiving enemy fire.

36. Night Medevac

The medevac standby mission calls for two Phrogs (CH-46s) and two Huey gunships (UH-1Es) or two Cobras (AH-1Gs) to position at the medevac standby pad on the west side of Marble Mountain airfield. After the aircraft are "set up" (pre-flight and pre-start checklists complete down to "battery—on," with the next step being "engine start—engaged"), then the crews "rack out" in the standby shed. The shed is equipped with a phone, radio, a radio operator and sufficient cots for all of the crew members to get some rest. The place is pretty nasty, hardly ever cleaned and, even then, not to a high degree of sanitation. Most nights, we don't get to spend the whole night there anyway.

Normally, each Phrog has five crew members—two pilots, a crew chief and two gunners manning the .50 caliber machine guns they carried as defensive weapons—and one of the two Phrogs would have a corpsman aboard to treat the wounded; each Huey gun had two pilots, a crew chief and a gunner (when fighting the enemy, the crew chief would man one of the two M-60 machine guns mounted as side-firing door guns). When a medevac call comes in, the copilots, crew chiefs and gunners head to the aircraft and complete the start sequence, prepping the aircraft for takeoff. Ideally, the guns would be ready to go as soon as the pilot was "strapped in." The pilots listen to the details of the call, take notes, check the large wall-mounted map, then head to the aircraft.

I had completed my flight restriction, but tonight I was flying as copilot with another great captain, who was a fairly recent addition to the squadron, in the lead gunship. The HACs of the two CH-46

The crews heading to the aircraft on the medevac pad.

helicopters and the command pilots of the two UH-1E gunships remained by the radios to get the specifics of the mission while the rest of us got the helicopters running and ready. My gunship and its twin were loaded for bear, each with four forward-firing fixed-mount M-60 machine guns, two seven-shot pods of 2.75-inch folding-fin aerial rockets with 17-pound warheads and two door-mounted M-60s manned by the crew chief and gunner. Little did we know that we would be calling for help and rearming and refueling several times during this mission.

As I got the rotors up to 100 percent, with the systems fully warmed up, the captain climbed in the pilot's seat, put on his helmet and said we were heading south. It was a fairly cool night, so I was able to get the aircraft into a low hover, ready to taxi for takeoff, while he hooked up his seat belt. With the armament and fuel load, we normally were not able to get into a full hover, just sort of scoot to a takeoff point or bounce along the runway until we achieved translational lift (the point where the aircraft is actually flying).

DASC had reported a Marine unit in a small village about 15 miles south of Da Nang was under attack and had several casualties that needed immediate medical attention. They were still taking fire from several directions and needed help.

I made the call: "Marble Tower, Comprise Medevac, a flight of two guns for immediate departure to the south from the medevac pad." The medevac pad has a lot of matting around it, so we would be able to bounce ourselves airborne as soon as we had clearance.

Tower responded, "Roger, Comprise. Cleared for takeoff. Report clear."

A few minutes later, "Marble, Comprise is clear south. Flight go, DASC."

"Two," came the response from our wingman. He was practicing strict radio discipline, with brief transmissions so as not to clutter the frequency.

At this point, the captain took over the radios and gave me precise instructions about where we were going. Then he called DASC:

"Da Nang DASC, Comprise medevac, clear Marble, en route Bravo 2-7."

DASC replied, "Roger, Comprise, Bravo 2-7 reports heavy fire from all quadrants, multiple emergency medevacs, standing by for extraction."

"Roger, DASC. ETA in ten. Requesting you launch 'Spooky' to work the west side of the village and put 'Basketball' overhead. We are going to need some light. Have them contact us on 252.2. Flight go squadron common." (Basketball was also a Marine KC-130 aircraft from

VMGR-152 that would loiter overhead and drop flares to illuminate the night sky, while Spooky was an air force C-117 fixed-wing gunship with multiple mini-guns and as much ammunition as can be loaded in a converted cargo plane.)

Again, our wingman replied, "Two."

Then, "Two is up."

"Roger, Two. Expect a racetrack east of the village running north to south, with a left pull. We'll bring the Phrogs in from the north, with a hard pull to the northeast coming out. We're going to try to light up that area."

Through the dark night sky, we raced down Highway 1, the Rolling Stones' "Honky Tonk Women" was blaring from the ADF. The north-south highway that ran from Da Nang through Chu Lai all the way to Saigon in southern South Vietnam split the village into east/west quadrants and an east/west river further divided it north and south. The bridge over that river was our planned extraction point since it had no railings or poles for lights or wires. It should be an easy spot for the Phrogs to land and load their medevacs.

I called, "Flight, go medevac common on FM." The frequency for medevac common on FM was 35.5, and the ground unit knew to be standing by awaiting our arrival on that frequency.

"Two," came the reply.

"Bravo 2-7, Comprise Medevac, overhead in about three mikes." (We used "mikes" as a shorthand version of minutes.)

"Roger, Comprise. This is Bravo 2-7. We are taking heavy machine gun fire from all quadrants and mortars from the northeast."

"OK, 2-7. We'll try to make your night a little quieter. We should have Spooky on station to the west in a few minutes. 'Peachbush Medevac' will be your transport birds. Expect them in about ten mikes."

As we approached the village, bright orange and red tracers rose slowly through the darkness expanding to the size of softballs, then seemed to streak by outside our helicopter's windows as the village below us suffered repeated explosions in the four quadrants formed by the east-west river and the north-south highway. The tracers that you could see added excitement, but our worries came from the four rounds between the tracers that you couldn't see. I was at the controls of our UH-1E Huey gunship maneuvering to position for a firing run, while the captain worked the radios, coordinating the arrival of the two medevac CH-46 Phrogs, setting up firing runs, confirming with DASC the arrival of Spooky, the U.S. Air Force AC-117 gun bird, de-conflicting traffic while watching out for where our wingman was and what he was preparing to do. It was going to be a long night. The Marines on the ground were reporting multiple emergency medevacs, and there seemed to be no end to the assault taking place.

The captain paused to yell over the intercom, "Hutton, if you hadn't screwed up your mission a few days ago, you could be flying wing instead of copilot. Then I could count on you to do what I need done. Instead, I'm concerned for what the rest of our flight is into."

The captain was partially right, of course. I had screwed up a mission, but my restriction to left seat was complete. It was only luck of the draw tonight that I was flying copilot. I was too busy to answer with more than a brief "roger." I was focused on putting some rockets into the mortar firing position northeast of the village, while avoiding return fire. I really didn't have time to tell him that I had cleared restriction, and it was just luck of the draw that I was flying copilot. I had the Huey in a slight dive, power on, ball centered and sights aligned as I squeezed off a pair of aerial rockets at the troubling mortar position (our choices for rockets were singles)—one rocket each time the trigger is pulled, pairs—one rocket from each pod each time the trigger is pulled or salvo—pairs of rockets in sequence until all seven rockets from each pod were fired with a single trigger pull. The most efficient use of our ordnance was pairs. "Honky Tonk Women" had finished playing, and Creedence Clearwater Revival was starting up on the ADF (I almost always had some music playing, no matter what was happening outside the aircraft) as I pulled off to the left to avoid overflying the enemy position. I noted the rocket strikes, pleased to see that there were several secondary explosions. That should take care of that mortar problem for a while as I looked for my next target. We needed to get some 7.62 mm rounds into the multiple targets around the village from the four forward-firing M-60 machine guns mounted on our gunship. Much more enemy fire needed suppression before the Phrog start hauling medevacs out of this hellhole. As I pulled left, I noted our wingman laying some rockets a little south of the mortar position, seeking targets that were active; our left-hand door gun was reaching out with fire from his '60, ensuring our pull was clear.

Spooky arrived on-site, reported in and immediately began putting thousands of rounds of 7.62 mm ammunition from their mini-guns into the hot spots and firing positions on the west side of the village. Basketball began their flair runs while I extended to the north anticipating the arrival of the Phrogs.

"Bravo 2-7, this is Peachbush Medevac inbound to the bridge. Stand by to load your casualties"; we will sequence in and out of the zone. "We can take about ten stretchers each load or fifteen ambulatories. Two, hold north until I pull," came the next radio call.

"Roger, Peachbush. Ready to load," was the ground unit reply. "Two" was his wingman's reply.

As the lead Phrog approached the bridge at 1,000 feet AGL to begin his spiral into the zone, I started a run on his blind side, putting a hail of bullets into the east outside the village, where I had seen some tracers originate. I crossed the nose of the '46 and pulled left as he settled onto the bridge.

Immediately, we heard the Phrog on FM: "2-7, load your first casualties."

"Loading now," came the reply.

We tried to time our firing runs with the arrival of the Phrogs, one of us in "hot" while the Phrog was landing and the other rolling in hot while he was starting his pull out, attempting to suppress fire so they could get in and out safely. We could see bright tracers racing in front of the nose of the CH-46 aircraft as it sat on the bridge loading casualties, so we focused our gun runs into the suspected origins of those tracers while the Phrogs continued loading.

Soon we heard, "Lead is pulling out left," followed closely by "Two's in." As the lead medevac 46 started pulling off the bridge, I rolled in on another firing run to cover their departure, and our wingman rolled in covering the medevac dash two into the zone. As soon as dash two had a load of injured Marines aboard, he pulled out on the same path as his lead.

As the flight of 46s left to deliver their critically injured Marines to "Charlie Med" each with a maximum load of medevacs, we raced back to Marble Mountain to rearm and top off the fuel tanks.

Because of the weight of the rockets and ammunition we carried, we were unable to take a full fuel load. So each time the '46s went back with their medevacs, we went to refuel and rearm. The way this night was going, it was important that we maintained as full a loadout of rockets and bullets as we could safely carry.

At Marble Mountain, our two gunships split up, with one of us going to rearm while the other refueled. In the arming pits, the crew chief and gunner loaded rockets into the pods and threw several cans of linked 7.62 mm ammunition in the back for the machine guns. The captain and I took turns unstrapping, climbing out of the aircraft and relieving ourselves. Once we finished rearming, we switched with our wingman and refueled.

Refueling was always an issue. The transports (Phrogs and Hogs) had a closed pressure refueling system, while ours was an open gravity system. That is, it was just like fueling your car; you stick a nozzle in the port on the side of the aircraft and squeeze the handle. We had to monitor the gauges closely so we did not take on more fuel than we could take off with.

When both aircraft had completed the cycle, we hustled back to the village to continue the rescue operation.

Over the course of the next five hours, we refueled and rearmed three times, each time returning to attempt to suppress more fire. The Phrogs evacuated over 70 emergency medevacs of both American and ARVN forces that night, proving the value of the air support.

The four aircraft commanders were awarded the Distinguished Flying Cross, while the copilots, crew chiefs and gunners each earned Single Mission Air Medals.

We were told later that a captured enemy soldier had a card on him depicting firing at a '46 (Phrog) by aiming in front of the flying aircraft. We figured that explained why we could see tracers zinging by the front of the Phrogs as they sat on the bridge loading medevacs. Fortunately, none of the aircraft or crews involved sustained any damage or injury. It was a long tiring night, but we were proud of what we were able to accomplish!

37

Section Lead

Not only is my suspension lifted, but I have been designated a section lead. My first flight as section lead is on June 12. The mission: armed escort for the morning and afternoon Rocket Belt VR.

On the 13th, I am back in a slick flying command and control on a VR and troop insert for the Seventh Marines out of LZ Baldy. My copilot is LtCol Bob Guay, the test pilot who looped and rolled the CH-53 during its initial acceptance. The insert aircraft are Phrogs escorted by two sections of Scarface Cobras. On the second team insert, the troops capture a suspected VC, whom they loaded in a departing Phrog.

Not long after the Phrogs depart to pick up another load of troops, the ground guys report a heat casualty. We pick him up and return him to the medical facility at LZ Baldy for treatment, returning in time to pick up another heat casualty whom we also return to Baldy. The final insert is the command party, and as that wraps up, there is a reported third heat casualty. This time, the Phrogs are still nearby, so they collect him and return him to Baldy. The entire mission, though lengthy, was fairly quiet, with no enemy activity. These hot summer months are going to be a problem for heat, with all the gear the Marines wear when they go to the field.

In two days' time, I am back in this area flying a gunship, escorting some Phrogs doing a resupply. This turns into another seven-hour flight while the Phrogs carry gear to the sites where the Marines are patrolling, again without any interaction with the enemy.

The rest of the month is very typical, alternating from left to right seat and lead to wing as we escort various resupply, medevac and VR missions. On only one mission did we receive and return fire with the enemy; that was an emergency extract of a recon team in the western Arizona area.

38

Cold Cokes Served on a Mountaintop

Another sunshiny, summer day; the temperatures were going to soar early. I had finished my "special" assignment as "meritorious copilot" and was flying wing on RT. We were a section of guns escorting some Hogs who were resupplying several units west of An Hoa, where the ridgelines and mountaintops peaked above 3,500 feet, some as high as 6,000 feet.

The normal procedure when a unit asks for an air mission is that they put in their request for what has to be done. The assignment of air assets then is made at MAF, so the unit does not always know what aircraft they are going to get for their mission. The supplies, mostly food, water and ammunition, were being staged as sling loads for the transport aircraft; each load was a couple of thousand pounds. The weight of the sling loads was well within the capability of CH-46 aircraft, but because this mission had CH-53s assigned, the loads were pretty light for the capability of the aircraft. It also meant that both '53s would have to go into each zone, which would double the risk.

The units were all in fixed locations and had not reported any enemy activity in the last day or two. With this quantity of supplies going out, the receiving units were all company-size encampments. We should not have the problem we normally encountered with small patrols from the Seventh Marines—that is, finding them. The regiment had good coordinates for each company, so the only reason for popping smoke will be to see wind direction instead of using the smoke to locate the unit. Because the NVA units monitored the radio frequencies, we had developed a specific sequence for identifying units by smoke. We would call for smoke to be "popped"; the unit would report, "smoke's out." Then we would call out the color of the smoke we could see. When the NVA was up to their tricks, we might have two or three different smokes showing

38. Cold Cokes Served on a Mountaintop

up, so we would respond with, "I've got green, red and yellow smoke." The unit would then confirm which color they had thrown out. Sometimes, not often, we would have to repeat the sequence a couple of times to narrow down the correct unit position.

We briefed with the '53 crews at Marble Mountain before departing and planned on heading to An Hoa before them, where we would top off our fuel and get the list of coordinates and frequencies for the units receiving supplies. The '53s had a better fuel-load capacity and significantly higher airspeed than we did, so it would be necessary to get ahead of them as much as possible.

The first four or five loads went like clockwork. We raced ahead of the '53s, established contact with the receiving unit and identified the zone, then escorted each of the '53s into and out of the zone. The only delays were caused by the ground troops clearing the first load of supplies out of the zone before the second '53 dropped his load.

The last load got interesting. The zone was well west of An Hoa, well up into the Que Son mountains. This time, the load was going into a small observation post located on the peak of a ridge above 3,500–4,000 feet elevation. The landing zone was about 15 yards from cliff to cliff, straddling the ridge, with the troops spread out laterally on both sides of the zone. They were only getting a small load of supplies. I reminded the '53 driver to drop his load quickly and move out using minimum power. Several weeks ago, we had resupplied this particular outpost, and the rotor wash from the '53 had caused an improvised "outhouse" the Marines had constructed to be blown a few yards off the side of the zone. Unfortunately, their lieutenant was inside at the time. We certainly did not want to repeat that event.

We got there just ahead of the transports, established communication with the ground unit and prepared to cover the '53 as it dropped off the supplies. The drop went quickly, without surprise (the Marines had moved their outhouse as far from the zone laterally as it could possibly go). As "Dimmer" pulled away, we got a call from the ground unit, relaying the information that part of the resupply had been some cold Cokes, well more than they could drink before they became too hot, and inquired if we wanted some of them. It had been a very hot day, and we were pretty tired, so RT responded, "Sure, I'll drop in and pick them up."

RT set up a gentle "no-hover" approach to the zone and touched down without incident. The Marines in the landing zone handed him some Cokes for his crew, while I orbited the zone. It seemed like it was taking RT a little long to get out of there, when I got the call from him, "Comprise 11, I can't hover to get airborne. I can't even get light on the skids without drooping turns." (Drooping turns is an expression for losing rotor revolutions for minute when applying power to the aircraft.) We had not expended any ordnance on this mission and had topped off our fuel tanks during our last stop at An Hoa. RT was well over his maximum gross weight to hover at this altitude and temperature. His only option to get off this hilltop was to get lighter.

There was no way he was going to leave his rockets and M-60 ammunition here, so something else had to be off-loaded. The solution was, as it turned out, for his copilot, crew chief and gunner to exit the aircraft. Then by carefully applying power, he was able to bounce the aircraft to the edge of the landing zone, and with one last bounce, he "jumped" off the cliff that marked the edge. As he descended, he was able to get into translational lift and fly the aircraft.

Now the real embarrassing part. We had to call the '53s to come back to the zone, pick up his crew and take them to An Hoa where he could pick them up. RT made the call, and the '53s returned. Fortunately, we still did not encounter any enemy activity. After the pickup, we followed the '53s to the airfield, and RT was able to get his crew back. He never told me how he enjoyed the Coke, and I certainly was not going in to get mine. We now owed the '53 crew a couple of drinks back at the club.

39

Recon Rescue

There are few guys that hang it out further than recon Marines. They deploy way out in the jungle; they travel in small groups (usually four to six) and are without support: no machine guns, no artillery, no mortars, just what they can carry or have delivered (by air—there's no Dominoes out here). You've got to love these guys; these are the guys with the big brass ones! Their motto: Swift, Silent, Deadly. We non-politically correct wise guys in the wing, after more than a few trips to the jungle to bring them home, made a small modification to their motto: it was now "Swift, Silent, Surrounded." Most of their movement is at night—that's when we are called to help.

As happens in the wing, we play as hard as we work, sometimes a little harder but only after all the standard missions are covered—the night stuff, two gunships to support night medevac and two guns to support Mission 80, the fast-reaction standby designed to support any special calls for unplanned action 24 hours a day. Once all the support aircraft are recovered and any test hops (post–maintenance inspection) completed, we were free to pursue leisure activities. These activities usually involved massive quantities of alcohol. After all, prices at the clubs were supportive of heavy drinking. We always followed the rules, though: no smoking within 12 hours of flying, no drinking within 50 feet of the aircraft. At least that's the way I remember it!

Bands at the club came in two flavors: Filipino bands imitating most any other band or group except country and an American band playing country music. I wasn't a true country fan, but I would stay just to see and hear an American band. This particular night, it was a true country band from the United States, and I hung around, drinking and enjoying myself.

Later, I was sleeping it off, when at two o'clock in the morning, the duty driver came in my hooch and shook me awake. He said, "Sir, recon is surrounded. They've got a medevac, and you've got to launch."

"Mission 80 is already deployed, and the medevac package are already out on separate missions. You've got to go!" I told him I had been at the club until after 11:00 p.m. and was in no shape to fly. He explained that the command knew that, but I had been one of the first to leave. When I asked whom I was flying with, he told me the name, which I recognized as one of the FNGs. Now I knew I was flying as aircraft commander, so I asked who flight lead was. His response, "You are, sir." Oh crap, this is going to be a long night! I climbed out of the rack, jumped into a flight suit, grabbed my web belt with sidearm and buck knife and headed out. My helmet bag, survival gear and body armor were already at the squadron.

We gathered up the rest of the crew and went to the squadron

Me (back to camera) playing Acey-Deucey with Lt Ellis "Tex" Nelson while on standby.

39. Recon Rescue

where we were briefed. Recon had been inserted 20-something miles west of Da Nang early in the morning, had some minor enemy contact and had started moving. The movement continued into the night, and one member of the squad had received a non-combat injury. They wanted us to pull him out, and they would continue their mission. We conducted a quick but thorough brief, checked in with the Phrog squadron that was providing the extract aircraft picking a place to rendezvous, pre-flighted our gunships and launched into the night. Weather in the area was reported as iffy; the fog was not just hazy eyes from the late club departure. Recon and whatever else we might find, here we come.

We got out ahead of the Phrogs, racing to the rendezvous point. Once we heard the '46 crews come up on the common frequency, we made radio contact with them. The farther west we went, the worse the weather was. At some point, the weather deterioration was going to cause problems; there was no way we could cover the flight of two Phrogs going into that area with these low ceilings and maintain visual contact between aircraft. I decided to leave the Phrogs and my wingman behind, orbiting a known point, and continue the approach to the landing zone with my single gunship. Nearing the zone, I made radio contact with the recon unit. We were still about a mile out from their position and closing as fast as conditions would allow. They were hiding just south of an acceptable landing zone. My plan was to sneak in, load the injured Marine and get out as quickly and quietly as possible. Recon would then continue movement on their mission.

Like overwater, sound in the jungle carries quite far, so the recon leader was whispering on the radio. With the volume on max, I could just make out what he was saying. When I asked how close the contact with the enemy was, I learned being a wiseass is not just an air wing trait. His response: "Why, do you want to talk to one of them?" I told him no, that was fine; we are inbound for extract. The deteriorating weather required that we get low and slow. Our approach to the landing zone was actually a low-level (near ten feet AGL) hover up the nearby river. As we came abreast the landing zone, I called for a flair or strobe. Recon replied, "Strobe out." As I broke over the tree line into the clearing, I could just see the flash of the strobe. I settled into the landing zone while the recon team ran from the tree line carrying the injured Marine. As quickly as possible, we loaded him into the Huey. As the remaining recon Marines disappeared into the tree line, I lifted into a hover and departed the zone exactly opposite the way we came in. We quickly cleared the area without receiving fire from the NVA, and the recon team was able to keep moving before the enemy had a chance to locate them. We worked our way back to the rendezvous point, continuing to fly at a very low level and joined our wingman and the Phrogs, then headed back to Da Nang. After dropping the injured Marine at the naval hospital medevac pad known to us as "Charlie Med," we returned to the base, shut down and returned to our respective hooches to catch some much-needed sleep before we had to be back on duty.

The entire mission had been completed in just over two hours from being pulled out of our racks. No enemy contact, no holes in the aircraft or any of the Marines. All in all, not a bad night except for the expected hangover! It was one of many missions accomplished where we were glad there were no breathalyzers available.

40

Recon and Tigers—Oh My!

Supporting recon was always an adventure, even when everything went according to plan. Recon's lives and their mission depended on getting into and away from the landing zone as quietly as possible. Unfortunately, there is nothing quiet about a helicopter. The inserts are done with Phrogs (or sometimes Hogs) with a two-plane gunship escort. There is definitely nothing quiet about that; we beat the air into submission, and that is a noisy process.

Uncle Milty (aka Lt Milt Matthews, Comprise 32) tells the story of one not-so-typical insert. The first part was very ordinary: a quick phone brief with the Phrog squadron, with a promise to do a face-to-face at An Hoa when they picked up the recon team.

Once the flight got to An Hoa, they ensured fuel tanks were full (as full as they could be with the load of ordnance we always carried, which meant we were usually limited to around 1,200 pounds of fuel—a full tank was 1,600 pounds); we had a full load of rockets and plenty of 7.62 ammunition for the machine guns.

When the flight crews met with the recon team, it was confirmed the preferred landing zone was pretty far west but still in country (that is, still in Vietnam); the area was rugged jungle with a few clearings. They identified primary and secondary insert sites and primary and secondary extract zones for each of the three days the recon element expected to be out there.

The flight outbound was about 35 minutes west; the terrain was rising and rugged. Once the zones had been spotted, with no apparent enemy activity, the Phrogs made an approach to a fake zone, then the real zone and one more approach to another fake zone. A quick radio contact with the team indicated all was well: no signs of NVA or VC and the team was moving out. The guns rendezvoused with the Phrogs and headed east. So far, no ordnance had been expended, and there was plenty of fuel.

Uncle Milty said they had been headed east toward An Hoa for about 15 minutes, still monitoring the recon frequency, when they got a call. Recon said that they needed to be pulled out and they would be in the primary insert zone. His thought was, "What the hell? They've gotten into a sh*t sandwich pretty quick." So the flight made a quick turn and headed west at top speed. Before they got to the zone, they inquired as to the enemy situation. The reply was surprising: there had been no enemy contact, but the ground unit had been forced to make some unintended noise that would attract the enemy. Milt responded that they were inbound and to stand by for extract.

Arriving over the zone, recon noted that there still had been no enemy contact, and they were ready for extract. The first Phrog made an uneventful approach, and as soon as they lowered their ramp, the team came out of the tree line with a large dead tiger suspended by its legs on a pole.

When everyone was back on the ground at An Hoa, the recon team reported that soon after they started moving, the tiger was spotted "stalking" them. The team opened fire on the tiger, resulting in a very dead tiger. Unfortunately, the gunfire was sufficient to give away their position to the enemy, so they elected to be extracted and would reset

The tiger that stalked a recon patrol.

the mission for another day. Uncle Milt thought the real reason for the extract was so they could bring the tiger back to base to show their buddies. After all, what good was a "war" trophy if you couldn't show it to anybody?*

---

* As related to the author by Lt Milt Matthews by phone, March 2024.

41

How to Become the O Club Officer in Two Easy Steps

The UH-1Es that we flew in HML-167 were very versatile aircraft; we could do anything (we thought), depending on fuel and weapons load, weather, overall gross weight and ignorance of (ignoring) restrictions. We were an excellent gunship, troop carrier, VIP support and emergency medevac aircraft. While we were an excellent gunship, the Cobras were awesome. They carried more ordnance and could deliver it with greater accuracy. They were faster getting to the zone. Their maneuverability around the zone really makes them a superior gun platform. Their ability to protect the transports and quell an enemy attack was unmatched. While we thought the AH-1Gs were good, you should see the AH-1Z, Viper, aircraft of today. But even they can't carry a medevac out of a hot zone or a zone fogged in by bad weather, right?

We've done that; bad weather doesn't keep a Huey out of a zone. I know from personal experience. If the weather is so bad that you can't cover the transports, you can still get a single Huey, even a Huey gunship, in the zone to pick up a critically injured Marine. I've done it, and so have others. The availability of helicopters to get Marines to a hospital has greatly reduced the fatality rate for Marines in combat. With helicopters available, the casualties of World War II would have been a fraction of what they were.

HML-167 with Huey guns and HML-367 with Cobras took turns being the escort aircraft for the medevac standby mission. Day and night, we (167 and 367) were always there. When the call comes, we launch. For this mission, the Cobras of 367 were on deck. A Marine was critically wounded in the mountainous area west of Da Nang. The weather was crap, but everybody launched, the Cobras out front, led

41. How to Become the O Club Officer in Two Easy Steps 167

by a captain and, in his front seat, a lieutenant that I had known from army flight school. We lived near each other in the "zoo," that raucous street full of Marine lieutenants with extra money in their pockets and a nearby liquor source, located just behind the officers' club at Hunter Army Airfield.

The deeper the flight got in the Que Son mountains, the worse the weather was. Eventually, they could go no farther as a flight. The captain in the lead Cobra had his wingman and both Phrogs orbit short of the pickup point, while he scouted ahead, hoping to find a path in. The Marine was critical; without immediate medical attention at a proper facility, he would die. As the captain proceeded, in radio contact with the ground force, he was hovering up the side of the mountain. He soon realized there was no way to get the transports in here. After a quick discussion with his copilot, they made the decision to continue; they had to try something unique in the history of the Cobra.

Arriving at the landing zone, he landed and had the ground troops bring out the injured Marine. His copilot exited the aircraft and assisted the troops while they strapped the injured Marine in the copilot's seat in the front of the Cobra, then locked the wounded Marine's harness so he couldn't move around and wouldn't fall on the flight controls. The copilot then climbed aboard the stub wing structure that holds the rocket pods on the side of the aircraft.

With everybody in place, Capt Roger lifted off, reversed his hover down the side of the mountain. As soon as he got into some clearer weather, he located a landing area and transferred the medevac into one of the '46s. The Phrogs headed to the hospital pad, and the Cobras went back to base to reconstitute the medevac package.

The word spread quickly. The squadron commanding officer had to meet with the group commanding officer. All things considered, something had to be done. The captain had done something nobody had ever done before, and because it had not been done, there was not a published restriction or procedure. (Nearly all restrictions come from something tried and failed, and all procedures come from something tried and succeeded.) The brass were in a quandary: behavior like this could not be allowed to continue, but he had saved a life. The choices—award him or ground him. If the outcome was to give him an award, would someone else attempt the same feat? If he was grounded, would there be a revolt? Word had already come from the ground side, to division, to MAF to wing and back down to the group. Division was happy that someone had taken some initiative to save a Marine. MAF and wing were happy that division was pleased, but MAF and wing were concerned about the risks the pilot took, both to the copilot and the aircraft. The final decision—give him a medal and a warning. In stern words he was told, do not repeat this action at great personal peril.

At the club, we just took this as another reason to celebrate with a few drinks. Roger (the captain pilot) and Dave (the lieutenant copilot) were the toast of the town, today's heroes. But what will you do for us tomorrow? That question was soon settled when Roger was back on medevac standby. The weather was crappy again. And Roger did it again, albeit with a different copilot and a slightly different outcome. He did save another Marine, but he earned not a medal but a new primary duty. He was now the officer in charge of the officers' club.

42

Guns, Guns, More Guns and Some Slick Hops

Coming off 88 hours in June (actually, a little more—I launched on a gunship escort on June 30 and that time was counted in July), I thought I might get a little break. Didn't happen! Jumping right into the fire, I was section lead on the medevac mission the night of the 1st where we launched five times to pick up seven critically injured Marines, returning to base at 0630.

Then on the 2nd, I flew section lead on the escort for the afternoon Rocket Belt VR, followed closely by flying the low bird on the 3rd and 4th. On the 4th, the area was unworkable (weather) and our flight of three was diverted to An Hoa to stand by for an emergency extract of some recon Marines. En route, we spotted a rocket pod lying in shallow water along the river. We landed, retrieved the pod and found that it still had six intact rockets loaded with white phosphorous warheads and one empty tube. We then took it out to sea and dumped it in deep water. (If that had ignited in the aircraft, it would have made for a very interesting Fourth of July celebration.)

On the 6th, I'm flying wing on the night medevac escort package where we launched six times to evacuate seven casualties. Now I get a couple of days off. Then on the 9th, I've got a seven-hour-plus single-pilot mission supporting the ROK Marines. Flying for them is always busy as they are constantly moving people around and we are the only way they can get their troops back to Da Nang for their end-of-tour rotation.

The Seventh Marines (Seventh Marine Regiment) are always lost. On the 10th, we spent almost seven hours in the air escorting the resupply Phrogs. A significant portion of that time was spent verifying their location before bringing in the supplies. That was all done south and west of Baldy and LZ Ross. Three days later, I'm right back in the same area, bringing more supplies to the Seventh Marines; this time, I'm copilot on Marvelous Marv's wing. Maybe the map-reading skills of the Seventh Marines are getting better: it didn't take us as long to finish the resupply, or maybe they hadn't moved very far. In the middle of this mission, we slip over to An Hoa and briefly escort a short resupply effort for the Fifth Marines.

The 14th and 15th, I am flying a slick command-and-control aircraft with a recent arrival as we accomplish multiple troop inserts and a command party into an area north and west of An Hoa for the Fifth Marines. The inserts on the 15th are ARVN troops going in to augment the Fifth Marines and eventually take over that area.

On the 16th, I am the copilot on the low bird with Big Al for the afternoon Rocket Belt VR. Amazingly, I have now gone through 16 days of July and not been shot at. The only shooting we have done was some crew training on the second. On the 18th, that was about to change.

We were flying the Baldy medevac package (gunship escort), and I was copilot with RT in the lead gunship. We were just pulling off a simulated gun run on the last medevac of the day when the ground troops informed us that we were taking fire. As the Phrogs came out of the zone, we rolled in hot, putting our 14 rockets in the suspected tree line, followed closely by our wing who put his rockets in the same general location. We both made a couple more runs with guns working up and down the tree line and expending about 6,000 rounds of 7.62 ammunition. Don't know if we hit anything, but the area got really quiet. While in the area, we covered one quick resupply mission, then returned to base for the day.

43

The Squadron Duty Officer

The squadron never sleeps. However, the commanding officer and his senior staff do occasionally leave for one reason or another, like getting some sleep, getting a haircut, eating a meal or just taking a break (remember what I said about the officers' club). The structure of the command does not change. When the commanding officer is gone, some lucky officer gets to stand duty as the squadron duty officer (SDO). He is the direct representative of the commanding officer in his absence.

Our squadron population of lieutenants varied from 30 to 80 officers during the year. Six or eight of these officers were assigned to the operations department and were tasked with preparing the flight schedule each night and stood a rotating duty during the day as the operations duty officer (ODO). They were excluded from the pool of potential SDOs. Those lieutenants who were designated as "department heads" were also excluded. That duty was then shared by the rest of us. Fortunately, with the multitude of officers checking into and out of the squadron during the year, I remember serving as the SDO only a few times throughout my tour. Whenever you had the duty as SDO, you were excluded from the flight schedule that day and the next, since it was doubtful that you would get any rest. It was not a desirable duty assignment. We were there to fly!

There is not much for the SDO to do for most of his tour of duty other than be ready to represent the commanding officer in his absence. Even though you didn't do much, you had to be nearby while others left for various reasons.

The ODO remains on duty until all the aircraft from the day's flight schedule have been recovered, even then the ops department remains busy until the next day's flight schedule is written and distributed. Most scheduled flights recover between 5:00 p.m. and 8:00 p.m. The aircraft assigned to the wing and division commanding generals

Uncle Milty on the left standing ODO with Lt Warren North.

and the chief of staff of III MAF rarely return later than 9:00 p.m. Most of the schedule is written by 10:00 p.m. and ready to go to print, pending receipt of any special assignments. Those are usually received by 11:00 p.m., and the schedule finished and distributed between midnight and 1:00 a.m. After that time, the only flights out are the medevac and Mission 80 standbys.

The last time I remember standing SDO was midsummer 1970. We had lost a single aircraft that day to a malfunctioning fuel system resulting in a fire. None of the four crew members had survived and recovery efforts were underway to retrieve their bodies. It was a painful day. It was going to get worse. Lt Lynn Boyer, Comprise 71, recalls the flight this way:

> As for the mission, it was a routine sniffer (APD). I don't remember exactly where, somewhere north and west. The area had been hit with a lot of Agent Orange, so a lot of it was defoliated. There were the typical mountain spurs that were triple canopy which we would fly up and down. Anyway, I was the pilot in command (PIC) in the sniffer bird with a copilot. Don't remember who the sniffer operator was. We were down in the weeds doing our treetop running when I heard the call of "FIRE" over the radio. If there was more, I didn't hear it. I thought we were being told we were taking fire, so I immediately turned and climbed at max power. We called asking where the fire was coming from and were told the low gun bird was on fire. We turned toward them, and they were burning from the cabin

43. The Squadron Duty Officer

area. Dave Geaslin, Comprise 33, was the PIC in the high gun and hollered at them that they were on fire and to shoot (fire their rockets to deny them to the enemy) and auto. The low bird, probably 500 ft AGL, started down with intense flames coming from the back of the cabin. Not long afterward, the tail boom departed the aircraft. Dick and Lew did a fine job shooting a tail boomless auto. They kept the aircraft level all the way down even though the fuselage had started to rotate slowly counterclockwise from torque. Just above the ground, they pulled pitch and arrested most of the descent, though expectedly the fuselage increased its rotation. The bird touched down level, skids collapsed though it remained upright, and the flames intensified to a red-white hot. I saw one of the crew move in the cabin fire for a couple of steps, then collapse. No one escaped. Dave Geaslin was extremely distressed and was going to try to land his gun bird and render assistance. I told him to stay airborne and I would land as I had the light bird. We started an approach to land; however, ammo and rockets started to cook off from the overloaded gunbird. The area was slight hills with sticks of denuded trees (from Agent Orange), and there was no place to land that was in defilade from the ordnance. We pulled up and off and circled. It was obvious from the intensity and extent of the fire that there were no survivors. The aircraft didn't explode, just burned white hot. Don't remember who called for medevac and assistance. I think Dave and his copilot were doing the calling and talking. They were high and had the range. Don't remember how long we circled, but after a while, our fuel started getting low (we had used a lot in the snooping and pooping), so we had to RTB [return to base]. I never did see the accident/incident report, but what I heard was speculation that the fuel line that ran under the crew cabin connecting the two fuel cells must have broken or someway leaked fuel into the spaces under the cabin. The fuel must have sloshed and spread through the space below the crew floor before igniting to have that extensive and hot a fire. Something ignited it, and then even though they were low, it was unrecoverable. They probably would have had to have been taxiing so they could do an immediate set-down and abandon the aircraft to survive.*

Sometime after 1:00 a.m., the schedule was written and distributed; all the other flights had been recovered. Everybody had gone to billeting; I was alone. I heard a vehicle pull up outside the squadron, a young Marine corporal walked in and handed me a small envelope and stated I was to hold it for the commanding officer. When I set it on the desk, the brittle paper split open and out spilled a scorched wedding ring and wristwatch. The driver then stated that this had been recovered from the crash site today and these belonged to the deceased pilot.

After my stint as SDO on the 19th, I didn't fly until the night of the

---

* As related to the author by Lt Lynn Boyer via email, January 21, 2024.

20th when I was assigned two consecutive nights of medevac escort, then escort for a resupply, followed by a day medevac.

Rest in Peace
1stLt Richard W. Dodd
1stLt Lewis E. Casner, Jr.
Cpl Johnny M. Rodgers
LCpl John F. Bennett
July 19, 1970

44

Twenty-Four Coke Grenades

Crew chiefs are an ingenious and sneaky lot; they bear watching at all times. They always have a bag of spare parts, a few extra bullets, anything they can get on the aircraft to make their life easier—sometimes a little too much. Speedy, our XO, was long gone; so, many of the artificial restrictions on our aircraft went home with him.

In the hot summer months after the monsoon season had completed, it could be difficult to get a loaded gunship airborne. With 14 rockets, a few cases of 7.62 mm belt-fed ammunition for the M-60s, two pilots, a crew chief and a gunner, our 1,600-pound fuel load might be limited to 1,200 or 1,400 pounds. On the really hot days, we would slide on the skids to the runway, then start out sliding into the wind with the crew chief and gunner outside the aircraft on gunner's belts, running along beside the aircraft as we bounced along. They would jump on the skids as we got to the last couple of bounces before hitting translational lift; then they would climb in and buckle up. We didn't do this too often, but sometimes it was necessary to get airborne and get the mission accomplished.

Knowing how much a crew chief would try to bring along, we always conducted a thorough pre-flight inspection. You never knew what excesses you could find and eliminate; three things we tried never to go without—adequate fuel, a full load out of rockets and as many bullets as we could bring.

Back in the '50s and '60s, Coke (the soft drink kind) was sometimes sold in 6-ounce or 8-ounce glass bottles and was distributed in a wooden case that held 24 bottles. One day while conducting the pre-flight inspection of my aircraft, I spotted a wooden Coke case under the bench seat in the back of the aircraft, nestled among the cases of ammunition we usually carried.

Being a curious sort of pilot, I examined the case a little closer and found, to my amazement, it was filled with hand grenades stuffed in

"Dixie cups." When I queried the crew chief, he explained that he had acquired the wooden case, got some hand grenades from the armory, put them in Dixie cups, with the safety pins pulled, and placed them in the wooden case. His plan was to dump the hand grenades out of the case while we were shooting at the enemy. The wind would pull the Dixie cups off the grenades. The spoons (on a hand grenade, the spoon is the lever that keeps the grenade from arming and starting its countdown to explosion) would then fly out, and three to five seconds later the grenades would explode, raining metal fragments over the enemy position. We were about to become a UH-1 bomber.

The one element the crew chief had failed to consider—wind blowing through the aircraft as we flew along, and it did get very breezy in the aircraft. I wonder what effect that wind would have had on the Dixie cups holding the hand grenade spoons in place. It could have gotten real exciting in the back of that aircraft had I let him bring the grenades along!

(From left) My crew chief, Cpl D Gonzales, me, my gunner, LCpl R Hernandes, and Lt Bill Graham.

45

Oil Can Bombs

Several of our daily missions required a single Huey slick (no aircraft armament—we still carried our individual service weapons but no crew-served or aircraft-mounted weapons). Usually, but not always, we were chased by a single CH-46 (Phrog). The runway at Marble Mountain was oriented generally north-south. When we launched north and had to turn west, we were immediately in the traffic pattern for Da Nang AFB, so as we transitioned west, we had to stay low, usually 50 feet or below until clear of Da Nang air traffic. Just south of the air force base and west of Marble Mountain, there was a river that ran east and west, and on the west side of Marble, the river ran south to north. Whenever we had to transition to the west, we followed that river. By being over the river, we could get low; we certainly didn't want to get in the way of the jet traffic.

Slick missions west of Da Nang included VIP support of the wing and division commanding generals. Pretty much all other flights could turn east and depart to the south to get where they needed to be. The river south of Da Nang usually had lots of sampan traffic on it. Fishing along the river fed a lot of families in the area of the city of Da Nang, but not all boat operators were loyal South Vietnamese fishermen.

The sampans on the river were very rickety; they didn't look like they could stay afloat, let alone support the small crew in them. On most of the boats, we could observe fishermen throwing their nets into the water and dragging them back, hoping for a good catch.

One bright day as we cruised along the river at low altitude, we observed a "fisherman" standing in his boat and firing a few rifle rounds at the aircraft just ahead of us. Because of the constraints of the traffic pattern coming out of Da Nang, we were committed to continuing our flight right into the lone gunman on the river.

Fortunately, our crew chief was prepared to take action as we passed over the boat with the gunman; he tossed out a quart can of engine oil. As I accelerated away from the boat, the aircraft behind us reported a direct hit on the boat; the can of oil had broken a hole in the bottom of the boat, and it was taking on water. The third aircraft back said that the boat rapidly sank, and the boat crew was swimming for shore.

For today, we really were a UH-1E bomber. I don't recall ever taking fire from any boats on that river for the rest of my tour in country.

On July 26, I began a new mission that would carry me through to the end of my tour.

46

III Marine Amphibious Force

At any given time, there were six Marine general officers in Vietnam: the commanding general (CG) and deputy CG, First Marine Division (1stMarDiv), CG and deputy CG, First Marine Air Wing (1stMAW), and CG and chief of staff, Third Marine Amphibious Force (III MAF). CG 1stMarDiv and CG 1stMAW were both major generals (two stars), and their deputies were brigadier generals (one star). The CG III MAF was LtGen Keith McCutcheon, and his chief of staff was BGen Tom Miller. General McCutcheon had been a groundbreaking helicopter pilot in Korea, and General Miller was known as the father of the AV-8 in the Marine Corps.

The commanders of division and wing were each assigned a Huey that would fly to their headquarters each day for whatever mission the CG required. The CG III MAF had a Huey and a specific pilot assigned that stayed at his headquarters 24/7. The helicopter only returned to Marble Mountain to take on fuel or for required maintenance. The CG III MAF also had a second Huey and pilot assigned that flew to the headquarters each morning to support whatever mission was required and would return to Marble Mountain when those requirements were complete. For my last couple of months in Vietnam, I was assigned that mission on a permanent basis. On most days, the CG released me and my aircraft to his chief of staff.

The chief of staff was a fixed-wing attack pilot and earlier in his career had helped introduce the AV-8B Harrier to the Marine fleet. Whenever we flew anywhere, he preferred to fly in the left seat (copilot's) and fly the aircraft. He had plenty of experience and was an excellent pilot, although I was still responsible for the aircraft.

I learned a lot while working for LtGen McCutcheon and BGen Miller. Both were fine officers who loved their country and served with honor. I got as close to General Miller as a lieutenant could without being his aide and was glad for the experience. I attended memorial services for General McCutcheon years later and was saddened to learn of General Miller's passing while researching material for this writing.

The next several stories occurred either while I was flying with one of the generals or to and from their headquarters.

47

Fishing the Explosive Way

The III MAF headquarters was located on the northwest side of Da Nang, just west of the approach corridor to the Da Nang AFB north-south runway and just slightly inland from the bay. The body of water on that north side was Da Nang harbor. Whether we flew in from the east (under the Da Nang AFB approach corridor) or the west, the approach required that we made a shallow turn over the harbor. There were always several small boats bobbing around in the harbor; usually, we could see a few people on the boats fishing with nets.

On any given day, the chief of staff would make several trips away from the headquarters, sometimes to the wing or division headquarters or the Korean regimental headquarters or to visit one of the many revitalization projects underway. After any of these trips, I would drop him at III MAF headquarters, then zip over to Marble Mountain to refuel. I learned early on to keep the fuel tank topped off since on one occasion I had failed to have the tank full, and the general had to wait on me instead of the other way around. He chewed my butt significantly that day: and I learned a lesson then regarding VIPs that I would never forget: You may and probably will wait at some point in the mission, but the VIP never waits on you! Prepare thoroughly; plan your fuel usage and any necessary stops. Ensure the VIP is *always* treated like a VIP.

On this particular morning, I had dropped the chief at his headquarters and headed to Marble Mountain to refuel. After fueling, I headed back to III MAF by flying north along the east coast, then turning west below the approach corridor before turning south into the landing zone. As I made the turn to final approach, there was a tremendous explosion just below the aircraft, spraying the bottom of the aircraft and tail boom with water. We were committed to the approach, so we continued into the III MAF landing zone.

After inspecting the aircraft for damages—there were none—we reported the incident to security forces at the headquarters. They quickly sent a reaction force via small boat to investigate and discovered that the fisherman in that boat had damaged his nets, so he had acquired some dynamite to use to aid his fishing. Unfortunately, either his timing or mine sucked. He scared the crap out of me. It could have had disastrous consequences for me if the aircraft had sustained serious damage or for him if we had been armed.

48

Orange Basketballs

Flying helicopters at night in Vietnam in the late '60s and early '70s was always an adventure. This was before night-vision goggles, and our Hueys had minimal stabilization equipment. Then there was always the risk of some bad guy taking a shot or two at you.

In the gunships, we were always lighting up the sky with outgoing tracers and the trail of departing rockets. We rarely had to make an approach to a landing zone—just pull off at sufficient altitude to make a safe recovery and not fly into your own frag pattern (the pattern of shrapnel thrown up by exploding warheads could easily inflict damage to your own aircraft if you were too low).

We didn't have the visual aids to fly low level at night, so we generally maintained about 1,000 feet AGL to and from our destinations. At night, that was plenty since the guys on the ground (good and bad) couldn't really see us. When we were shooting while escorting CH-46s into and out of "hot" zones, we usually had Basketball to light up the night sky with an assortment of flairs. When we had to make a night landing in the field, we had the guys on the ground throw out a strobe in the center of the landing area, then we would fly over at that 1,000 foot altitude. Once over the zone, we would roll the aircraft on its side, point the nose at the ground, and make a rapid descending 360-degree turn, arriving back over the intended point of landing at near-zero airspeed and altitude. We would set the radar altimeter warning light at five feet and stabilize in a hover there, then descend to the final landing. The first time you see one of these approaches as a copilot, it all happens in a hurry. And when the radar altimeter light comes on, it is quite a shock; you just hope the pilot has it all under control.

Anytime you flew at night, you could expect to have a few shots sent your way. Small-arms fire you never really knew about since most rifles weren't loaded with tracers. Small-caliber automatic weapons did have tracers and you could tell when they were firing your direction;

most times, they weren't a problem even though there were four rounds between every tracer that you couldn't see.

At any time, there were four to six Marine general officers in country and we hauled them around frequently. We had a Huey assigned to the division headquarters, another assigned to wing headquarters and two assigned to the generals at MAF headquarters. Returning from wing, division or MAF headquarters at night, we usually flew south on the west side of Da Nang AFB, then approached Marble Mountain south of Da Nang. Anywhere along this route, you could expect to have a few rounds fired at you and it was usually not a problem.

One night as I was returning from the MAF headquarters, I was flying south on the west side of Da Nang, about 500 feet, just me and my crew chief. As we got abreast Da Nang AFB, we started seeing these huge orange fireballs coming straight at the aircraft. We had no opportunity to take evasive action or respond in any manner; we were in an unarmed aircraft without escort at low altitude and in restricted airspace—nowhere to go.

The orange basketballs seemed to pass right by the aircraft in slow motion. The only thing that wasn't going in slow motion was my heart rate. We reported the incoming fire to Da Nang DASC, and it was later determined that the fire was coming from a 50-caliber machine gun. A reaction force that responded to the area had captured the gun and crew that had infiltrated the city of Da Nang.

When we got back to Marble Mountain, the aircraft was checked thoroughly for damage; none was found except for some webbing from the pilot seat that was sucked up my butt. I seemed to get shot at a lot, so the "Magnet Ass" nickname previously earned was bound to stick.

49

The Miss America USO Show

While we had many minor USO presentations at the officers' club in the form of Filipino bands imitating most Western rock bands, we also had two major USO shows during my year in country. The first was the Bob Hope show over Christmas 1969, and the second was the Miss America show featuring the 1970 Miss America and several of the previous year's state winners including Miss Texas and Miss North Carolina in August 1970.

Their show was conducted in the same amphitheater as the Bob Hope show and was a lighthearted song-and-dance routine featuring several of the state representatives, much to the entertainment of the thousands of young men who had not seen a "round-eye" for the better part of a year. Young men from the audience were brought on stage and got the opportunity to dance and generally make fools of themselves with the ladies in the show. It was all in good fun. No feelings were hurt, and many young men fell in love!

Shows were presented in Da Nang, Chu Lai and Phu Bai in I Corps as well as a number of locations to our south. We routinely used several Hueys and Phrogs to ferry shows to different locations, with different members of the show being distributed between the helicopters.

On one of the movements of the Miss America show, I had Miss North Carolina 1969, Patricia Johnson (now Gilliland), a student from Meredith College in Raleigh, in the left seat of my aircraft. Not everyone in the helicopter had headsets capable of communicating with the crew, but she did.

I was able to carry on a pleasant conversation with her as we flew and even let her handle the controls of the aircraft briefly. I already had my orders to MCAS New River in Jacksonville, North Carolina, for when I left Vietnam. So never being one to miss an opportunity, I asked

The Miss America USO show, with Miss America 1970 fourth from the left.

Our Hueys waiting to transport the Miss America USO show.

49. The Miss America USO Show

Patsy to be my date at the Marine Corps Birthday Ball in November 1970, and she accepted.

Unfortunately, the sad ending to this tale was that I was still in Missouri with my mother and father celebrating their 25th wedding anniversary when the time for the ball came and went. I tend toward procrastination and never made the effort to contact Miss North Carolina again, even though it would have been relatively easy to contact her through Meredith College, the USO organization or the Miss America organization.

Miss North Carolina, 1969, Patsy Johnson.

50

Overloaded Medevac

Major insertions or operations required senior officers to oversee or exercise command and control. As the exercise or operation grows in scope or complexity, the requirement for a very senior officer to direct it also grows. Within the aviation community, we usually assign a "mission commander" to coordinate the activities of the individual flights while accomplishing the mission. Once on the ground, the officer exercising command and control directs the ground units and responds to the requirements of those units.

When supporting command and control missions, we install a special console equipped with several ground- and aviation-compatible radios in the aircraft. We also include an additional crew member responsible for keeping the console operating properly. With the pilot, crew chief, operational commander and his staff aboard and a full fuel load, the aircraft is near its maximum weight.

On this mission, we were operating south and west of An Hoa, about 35 or 40 miles southwest of Da Nang. The chief of staff was in the left seat. We had the command and control console aboard with its operator, the general's aide and another ground officer. The day's temperature was quite high, which also limited how much we could carry.

About 40 minutes into the operation, we had most of a regiment inserted in the area. The Phrogs had departed to refuel, and a section of them would be on standby for any subsequent mission requirements. Two sections of Cobras were in a high orbit, prepared to provide fire support in the event of enemy contact. As command and control, we were listening to the ground frequencies, prepared to provide support as needed.

The troops on the ground were in full battle dress with flak vests and about 60 or 70 pounds of gear, including rations and water for a two- or three-day operation. The temperature and humidity were

50. Overloaded Medevac

continuing to climb, approaching black flag status for a training day. Unfortunately, this was not a training exercise; this was combat.

Shortly, one of the platoon commanders reported a heat casualty and required an immediate medevac. Our CH-46 troop transport aircraft were refueling and not expected back for the better part of an hour, and the medevac standby from Marble Mountain was already deployed on another mission. The chief of staff, BGen Miller, asked me if we could take the Marine aboard and transport him to Charlie Med. I said that it would be close but that we should be able to handle the weight.

The landing zone for the pickup would be on the western edge of a large clearing that sloped up from west to east. The ground forces popped a smoke to indicate the pickup point, and I set up an approach from west to east downwind with the light breeze, with the majority of the approach over areas the troops had already swept through. After landing, the casualty and his gear were squeezed into the aircraft.

There is a technique that we've used many times to get a heavily loaded gunship airborne. Once we are set up into the wind, we add power until the aircraft is light on the skids. Then we move the cyclic forward just enough to begin picking up speed. The aircraft slides along the ground and bounces a few times as it achieves transitional lift (that point where the aircraft transitions into flight). It works really well on a runway, sliding into the wind.

I kept the aircraft heading east and attempted a sliding takeoff through the clearing, with most of the Marines behind us to the west. We bounced and skidded along the grass for several hundred yards but never got into translational lift. Two factors were working against us: one, we were heading slightly uphill, and two, we had a light tailwind with a heavily loaded aircraft. As we came to a stop at the far end of the clearing, General Miller asked me if we were going to be able to accomplish this. I replied that we would, now that we were going into the wind and downhill. We needed to get out of this area before bullets started flying!

We made a careful turn and started sliding and bouncing into the wind, and within 100 yards or so and with one last bounce, we transitioned into flight. It takes a little less power to maintain flight than it does to hover, so we were good. I climbed to a safe altitude and headed to Charlie Med. After dropping off the casualty, we refueled and returned to the operation. By then, the Phrogs had returned and we were able to finish supporting the ground operation without any additional problems.

The ground troops continued their sweep through the area without further casualty and had little to no enemy contact. The Phrogs finished the insert as the troops continued the operation sweeping through the area. With the regiment fully in place, we were released, and I took the chief of staff back to III MAF headquarters. The regiment would remain in the area for the next couple of days and call for air support only as needed.

51

Returning the Navy

On many occasions, the CG III MAF or his chief of staff would host a dinner in the general officers' mess for various dignitaries and senior officers who were visiting the I Corps area. Each of these dinners tended to stretch into the night and usually involved some serious application of alcohol.

Most of these visits/dinners did not involve either of the two crews and aircraft assigned to III MAF headquarters as the various dignitaries had their own assigned transportation to their quarters or they were staying in VIP quarters at the III MAF headquarters. Occasionally, the visitor was from the navy and required air transportation back to their ship. Usually, the ships were just offshore or anchored in Da Nang harbor, which did not create a problem for us.

One time, however, things were a little more interesting. One of the dinner participants was a navy admiral who needed to be returned to his ship. Unfortunately, the ship got underway about three hours before the dinner and visit was complete. The ship was making about 15 knots, so it was about 45 nautical miles out to sea before we could start that direction. At our predicted airspeed, the ship would move three to four miles farther away for each 15 minutes we had to fly, so we would be chasing a moving target. Still, this wasn't normally much of a problem.

Night overwater flight is instrument flight; there is no horizon, no visual reference of any sort. Flight in Vietnam was not like flight in the States; there was no radar following, no big brother on the ground watching out for you, nobody expecting you back at any certain time. You were on your own, flying instruments, watching attitude, altitude, airspeed and direction, following your TACAN needle. As we departed the III MAF landing zone, we climbed to 1,500 feet and headed into the night, my vision firmly fixed on the instruments available to me, scanning, observing any deviation in course, altitude, attitude or any other phenomena that might disrupt our flight and plans.

A quiet flight at night is filled with noise. What are normal aircraft noises during the day become harbingers of doom at night. As we flew along, we had those noises, the rattles, the shakes, the vibrations, but we could find nothing wrong, no reason to turn back, so we proceeded.

Night overwater flight was still not the worst of our problems. Most amphibious support ships have a large open deck at the stern of the ship which has minimal impact from prevailing wind on your landing. The ship's superstructure is designed to minimize the effect it has on the wind over the landing area. Helicopter landing ships, like LHAs and LPHs, and aircraft carriers have a huge deck for landing and parking multiple aircraft and can turn directly into the wind, so the helicopter can land into a direct headwind or at least a minimal crosswind. Even the landing area on the hospital ships USNS *Repose* and USNS *Sanctuary* was located aft of the superstructure. Not so tonight!

The ship we are heading to tonight was an older model heavy cruiser and had an unusual configuration. While the landing platform was located on the aft portion of the ship with superstructure forward, it had a large crane located aft of the improvised flight deck, which impacted the approach to landing. Ideally, the ship's captain would turn the ship 45 degrees to the prevailing wind and slow to 5 or 6 knots. As I approached the ship, I would have to slide the aircraft to the right, matching the ship's speed and control the helicopter to compensate for the burble coming off the forward superstructure.

As we headed east into the night, we were getting a headwind of about 10–12 knots, which was increasing our flight time to the ship. The night was overcast, without a moon or stars. I expected to arrive at the ship when it was about 60 nautical miles offshore. The flight was smooth enough at about 1,500 feet altitude, and I was able to start receiving the

The USNS *Repose*, note the landing area on the aft portion of the ship.

51. Returning the Navy

TACAN navigation signal from the ship when I was only about 35 miles away. So far so good!

I contacted the ship about 20 miles out and was assured she would slow to 5 knots and turn slightly so the wind was 45 degrees off the starboard bow. I would be able to make a nearly straight-in approach. About seven miles out, I started picking up the lights of the ship. Primary flight control reported a rough sea state with swells of 10–12 feet. This older model ship was not equipped with any stabilization equipment, so this landing would be a little touchy.

At three miles, I was cleared to land and could see the lighted wands of the landing signal enlisted—a sailor with lighted signal wands who would assist us with the landing. The swells were coming at the ship as it pretty much aligned with the wind, so the ship was both pitching and rolling. This landing was probably going to be more of a controlled crash than a landing. I had the crew chief wake the passengers and ensure that they were ready to land, seat belts fastened securely. They had fallen asleep during the flight, probably from the alcohol consumed with dinner. Fortunately, I had had none.

With a little luck, I arrived over the landing spot just before the ship was reaching the apex of its roll. By planning on a nearly no-hover landing from a right sideslip and a plan to land as the ship reached its apex, I was fortunate that the plan worked, and I released power at that point and the aircraft touched firmly down on deck. As it turned out, it was a very smooth landing. The passengers departed, happy to be back aboard, never knowing how bad that landing could have been. It was mostly a combination of good luck, good fortune and being in the right place at the right time. I don't think I could have repeated that approach 2 out of 20 tries.

We topped off our fuel tanks, accepted some coffee from the navy and lifted off for the return to Marble Mountain without incident. As we turned to shore, with the lights of the ship disappearing behind us, we climbed back to 1,500 feet and headed home, this time with a tailwind helping shorten our trip. Flying toward shore is a little easier. As we got within 15 miles, we were able to make out the lights of Da Nang, continued our flight around "Monkey Mountain" and landed back at Marble Mountain Air Facility, totally ready to call it a night.

52

How High Can You Go?

Every once in a while, I was out flying with no place to go and nothing to do. Today, General Miller had me drop a VIP up at Phu Bai and then I would be released. We were returning via the Hai Van Pass to Marble Mountain with an empty airplane. My crew chief and I had chatted about the limits of our aircraft, specifically about how high we could fly. There was an established service ceiling of around 18,000 feet for the Huey. Flight above 18,000 feet is measured in "flight levels," not feet—that is, flight level 180 for 18,000 feet or flight level 220 for 22,000 feet. NATOPS said that above 12,000 feet, you had to be on supplemental oxygen; you could fly between 10,000 and 12,000 feet for short periods without supplemental oxygen, but you needed to be aware that you could suffer the effects of oxygen deprivation after about half an hour. The service ceiling was the point where the aircraft would not respond to control inputs properly. (There is always some margin of error there, but I had no idea what the margin was.)

In any case, we had time. We were already around 6,000 feet on our altimeter, which was about 3,000 feet AGL. Trying to stay out of range of small-arms fire, I had already been hit once (probably by accident or an extremely lucky shot) while cruising, so I didn't want to provide a target of opportunity to any stray VC who wanted to take a potshot. Who knows when they will get lucky again.

We reported to Da Nang ATC that we would be holding over the Hai Van for a few minutes. They requested that we notify them when we were back en route. So for the next 15 minutes, we climbed while circling. We were only getting 1,000- to 2,000-feet-per-minute climb rate, and the higher we went, the lower the rate got. As we passed 10,000 feet, the climb rate slowed but continued to show some progress. Through 12,000 feet, the aircraft continued, and through 14,000 feet, progress was really slow. That's where we decided to stop.

I radioed ATC that we were back en route and quickly descended.

52. How High Can You Go?

We came out of Hai Van Pass descending, traveled south, west of Da Nang AFB, then turned east to Marble Mountain once we were clear of Da Nang. The aircraft had been very sluggish at 14,000, but we now knew we could go there if we ever needed to.

53

Another Painful Loss

By now, I'm near my last month in Vietnam. I have my orders to MCAS (H) New River, Jacksonville, North Carolina. I will report to Marine Helicopter Training Group 40 (MHTG-40) after 30 days of leave and 8 days of allocated travel. My report date will be driven by the date of my flight out of here to Okinawa and then on to the States.

Today, I was released by the chief of staff early and returned to the squadron. I didn't have much else to do, so I hung around the ready room, played a little Acey-Deucey with some other lieutenants who were hanging out. Acey-Deucey is a Marine-modified version of backgammon. It has a little more movement, excitement and tactics involved.

The squadron radio broke through the boisterousness of the ready room with some alarming news. One of our gunships had been shot down about 20 miles south of the airfield. His wingman reported the situation where his lead had made a low pass on a clearing where a single individual was desperately waving at the flight. As he approached the landing zone, a tremendous volume of enemy fire erupted from the tree line, striking the lead gunship, which then crashed in the field. Dash two returned fire, and the Phrogs with them inserted some troops who proceeded to secure the area. The pilot, copilot, crew chief and gunner were all KIA. Their bodies were recovered by the troops from the Phrogs. Dash two had some damage and was returning to the flight line. The grunts were still on the ground and needed some gun support.

The ODO assigned me as flight lead for the reaction flight. We briefed, conducted the pre-flight and were airborne in about 20 minutes. The tension and anxiety were high. We were loaded for bear and intended to extract some payback. Each aircraft had two side-mounted crew-served M-60 machine guns, four fixed-mount forward-firing M-60s and two seven-shot 2.75-inch folding-fin aerial rocket pods, each rocket with 17-pound warheads. My left-hand pod was loaded with fléchette rockets. A fléchette rocket had about 150 steel arrows that

53. Another Painful Loss

were an inch and half long loaded in the warhead. These were best used against soft targets like personnel in the open.

As we approached the site, we made contact with the ground force and determined that the enemy was attempting to pull back to the west. The grunts were in a cautious pursuit, and as we came overhead, they would put on some more pressure. Once we had established the location of the lead ground force, we began strafing the trees west of them with our forward-mounted M-60 machine guns.

We moved west with the troops in hot pursuit. About 2,000 meters west of the initial contact, we came into another clearing. On the first pass, we spotted some enemy troops trying to move into the tree line on the west end of the clearing. I set up a firing run that would cross the tree line from north to south with a pullout to the east. On my first run, I selected pairs of rockets and rolled in hot.

Firing a fléchette rocket is a little different than a regular rocket in that the release or firing point has to be a little further out. If you are too close to the target, the warhead does not arm, and instead of exploding above the target and raining terror on the enemy, the rocket impacts the ground unexploded. The VC have been known to recover the unexploded ordnance and use it in booby traps against our troops. Earlier in the year, we had a major in the squadron provide seven of these warheads to the bad guys by shooting without sufficient time for the warheads to arm. So I was particularly careful to get my shots off early.

On my first run, I fired off three pairs of carefully aimed rockets and pulled off to the east. The fléchette armed properly and exploded about 100 meters out from the enemy. As I pulled off, my wingman rolled in placing three more pairs of rockets about 30–50 meters west of my run. On my second run, I finished off my rockets with four pairs, and my wingman did the same. As we pulled off, our door gunners were covering our pull with a continuous stream of 7.62 mm lead from their M-60s.

Reports of body counts seemed to fill the nightly news at home, both friendly and enemy. As gunship pilots, we never saw the results of our shooting; usually, we only knew that we had done a good job when friendly forces reported that they were no longer receiving enemy fire, or sometimes we could see secondary explosions from enemy armaments.

After our second run, the troops on the ground reported no more enemy fire and were able to sweep through the area, recovering several VC bodies and many wounded prisoners. They reported that some of the VC bodies had been stuck to a tree, like they had been stapled there. When you are the target of a fléchette rocket, it's like being hit by hundreds of tiny arrows.

By then, the Phrogs had returned and began extracting the ground forces and prisoners.

Upon returning to the squadron, I learned the pilot who had been killed was a friend who had arrived in country on the same aircraft as I and had his orders home in hand. He would have been leaving Vietnam in just a few short weeks.

Rest in Peace
1stLt Ralph N. Duemling
1stLt Joseph H. Shelton, III
Cpl David L. Smith
Cpl Thomas H. Peppenheim
August 18, 1970

54

Winning the Hearts and Minds

Over my last month in Vietnam, I came to realize a new perspective about the war and what was happening in country.

At least twice a week, either LtGen McCutcheon or BGen Miller would visit a civic action project that was underway in I Corps (the country was divided into several specific regions labeled as Corps, with I Corps being the northern section of the country). Whenever LtGen McCutcheon visited an area, both his primary pilot and chase crew went.

Some examples of projects that we observed included schools and villages being rebuilt, protected corridors around villages were constructed so that farmers were able to raise and harvest crops, small civilian airports in remote areas were being hacked out of the jungle, and in larger communities, schools, hospitals and clinics were being constructed. Where we could, Marines and civilian contractors were assisting with staffing, training of local tradesmen and, in general, preparing the area for a return to normal civilian life without a war.

LtGen McCutcheon and BGen Miller also met with local politicians, helping them to understand the political process, how to set up elections and a local government.

The August and September 1970 command chronologies for III MAF list the man-days (ten-hour days) provided in support of various civic action programs ongoing in I Corps totaling over 2,500 man-days for August and 1,700 for September. The institutions supported included over 40 schools, 20 orphanages and 20 hospitals. Civilian patients seen in military medical facilities from non-hostile injuries and illness totaled almost 40,000 for each of the two months and nearly 200 for injuries resulting from hostile action. Other projects listed included land clearing, road building and village reconstruction. The

(From left) Me, III MAF CoS BGen TH Miller, III MAF SgtMaj Skinner, and my crew chief Cpl KF Garrett.

Waiting on VIPs: (from left) Cpl McGaha, Maj Martin, me, Cpl Garrett.

54. Winning the Hearts and Minds

wing reported several animal husbandry projects, and the force logistics command detailed the construction of wells, a community bath, housing projects and a marketplace.

These things are just a few of the activities that were going on in the provinces of South Vietnam. If we had been allowed to continue, South Vietnam would be a free country today. For more details on civic action projects ongoing during my last few months in Vietnam, see Appendixes B and C.

When I got home, I learned from my parents and from various civic groups where I gave presentations that the things I had observed firsthand were not being reported in the media, although most news outlets were aware of them. Vietnamization was in full swing, and apparently, good news does not sell newspapers or commercials on TV.

55

Farewell Dinner

The end of my tour in Vietnam was fast approaching. I had my orders in hand, and my replacement as the chase pilot for LtGen McCutcheon had been chosen and trained. He had flown with me for the last several days, and tonight was to be my last day flying. Tomorrow, I would start my packing and arrange shipping for my personal belongs (read mini-fridge, TEAC tape deck, speakers, amplifier, reverberator and many tapes) and begin checking out of HML-167 and MAG-16. My orders were to take me to MCAS(H) New River, Jacksonville, North Carolina, having completed nearly 1,000 flight hours in combat with about 380 of that at night. I had earned 41 Strike/Flight Air Medals on over 820 combat missions and a Single Mission Air Medal for the night medevac mission described earlier. I was ready to go home. All I needed was my flight date and that should be between four days and two weeks.

At the end of the day's missions, LtGen McCutcheon and BGen Miller had invited me, my replacement and my crew chief to dinner in the generals' mess. It was an honor to be invited. The major I replaced had not been so honored. That night, we had a great steak dinner with baked potato, a salad and a little wine. It happened that there was a small USO band playing at the III MAF club after dinner, and the three of us (me, my replacement and my crew chief) went there, where we had a few more drinks and sang along to some great music.

We considered spending the night (recommended by BGen Miller) at III MAF headquarters and flying back the next morning, but we really hadn't had that much to drink (at least not when compared to some other daring night flights). After all, the "no smoking within 12 hours of flying" and "no drinking within 50 feet of the aircraft" rules were still in effect. We somehow managed to fly back without incident.

I planned on sleeping in until about 9:00 a.m., then start my checkout. That plan had a hole blown in it when I was awakened at seven in

55. Farewell Dinner

the morning by the duty driver, who stated that my flight date was in, and I had today to pack and check out. Tomorrow, I would be gone. I had to be at the processing center at Da Nang AFB by 1:00 p.m. That threw my day into a spin. I had to pack my personal belongings and arrange for shipping, then check out of both MAG-16 and the squadron quickly. Fortunately, the duty driver told me he was mine until I was gone. He helped me pack, took me to logistics and helped arrange for my stuff to be picked up.

I got to the processing center a little after one the next day, but they took care of me anyway. As it turned out, my flight didn't leave until after 7:00 p.m., so I had some waiting to do. While waiting, I ran into a master sergeant from MATCU-69. He had been a gunnery sergeant when I last saw him when I was a corporal in 1967. We talked for a while. He was just arriving in country and was waiting transportation to his unit. I learned that he was working on his application for commissioning and was going through the process to have some tattoos removed. I wished him luck and departed when my flight was called. My flight out took me to Okinawa for another short stay. This time, the returning veterans were not assigned any additional duties, and I was able to

An aged and experienced Lt Hutton about to head home.

visit with my friend from high school again. At the end of the week, I was assigned a flight to California, then caught a civilian flight to St. Louis, Missouri. I departed Vietnam on September 30, 1970, just over 11 months in country.

56

Home at Last
October 1970

My parents picked me up in St. Louis, and we enjoyed a great reunion. As it turned out, my parents were planning a celebration of their 25th wedding anniversary while I was home. The timing was not great; it would prevent my expected Marine Corps Ball date with Miss North Carolina. But I loved my parents, and I could certainly make this small sacrifice for them.

When I got home, I found that General Motors was on strike and that interfered with my intended purchase of a new car. After checking with the local dealers and several dealers in nearby cities, I was able to find a new 1972 Chevrolet Monte Carlo in stock in Salisbury, Missouri. It was a "curb-yellow" two-door sedan with a fake black vinyl top and would serve me well for several years.

I spent the next couple of weeks visiting friends and just generally catching up. I was invited to give a presentation to the local Kiwanis Club, which I did in uniform. As part of the discussion, I reviewed the civic action programs taking place in Vietnam and generally my view of how it was going. It was there that I learned how poorly the media was covering our efforts. What I did not see in the Midwest were the anti-war protests. They seemed to be countrywide if you watched the ABC, NBC and CBS version of the news.

A few weeks after I got home, I visited a female friend in Canton, Missouri, where my brother had attended college. He got married his senior year and had moved to Memphis to attend grad school.

I was able to stay with his in-laws while in Canton. The friend I visited was the former wife of one of my brother's friends whom I had met when I visited before leaving for Vietnam. My mom called me the second day I was there and asked that I fly into Chicago and pick up a Cessna aircraft that her boss had left there because of bad weather. My brother's in-laws took me to Quincy, Illinois, where I caught a commercial flight into Chicago Midway. It was late when I was able to get the aircraft (it was parked at Palwaukee Municipal Airport in Wheeling, Illinois) and I ran into darkness flying home. Normally, this wouldn't be a problem except that I was unfamiliar with this particular aircraft and couldn't find the switches for the cockpit panel lighting. I should have done some familiarization before launching; every time you fly, you learn something. Failing to retain that knowledge is the problem; retaining and recalling knowledge learned is the solution.

I was able to land back near Canton, Missouri, as the last light disappeared, and I spent another night with my brother's in-laws, then continued home the next day. This side trip required me to leave my new car in Canton in the custody of my friend.

My parents' 25th anniversary party was the next weekend, and on Friday, Dad and I flew Mom's company aircraft to pick up my brother and his wife in Memphis. After refueling in Memphis, the aircraft (a turbocharged Cessna 210) wouldn't start. After a little delay while the flooded engine cleared, I got it started, and we were off for Moberly and the party on Saturday. Unfortunately, the delay in Memphis caused us to still be en route well after dark and made the last 45 minutes of flying interesting as I tried to identify the correct airport without any terminal guidance. I had been so familiar with the terrain in Vietnam that I pretty much abandoned flight planning. I had better get it together fast or I would become a statistic. After spotting a lighted runway, I made a low pass and identified the airport as the one in Mexico, Missouri. Now that I knew where I was, the rest of the trip was simple. I followed Route 22 West to US 63, then 63 North to Moberly. No problem—a revised version of IFR, instead of "instrument flight rules," it became "I follow roads."

My Canton friend drove my car down for Mom and Dad's anniversary party and returned to Canton with my brother's in-laws. I was planning to fly my brother and his wife back to Memphis on Sunday, but the weather deteriorated to the point where they had to fly commercial.

A couple of days after the party, I was hanging around the local bowling alley having a couple of cold ones and ran into the miniskirted redhead I had met while making out my will. Although we talked for a couple of hours, I couldn't remember her name, but I did remember where she worked. The next day, I had my mother call her boss and ask her name and get her phone number. Then I called and asked her out again.

In the final days before I departed for my new duty station, we managed to squeeze in a couple of dates. I ran into her again several months later. I was home visiting. My grandmother was in the local hospital, and my parents and I were there visiting her. The redhead was there visiting a friend who had just had a baby. We visited for a while and later exchanged correspondence. Our visits became more frequent and much more serious through 1971. Then she and I married in April 1972.

57

Semper Fidelis

The title "Marine" is earned, never given. You don't join the Marine Corps; you join the army, navy and air force, but you *become* a Marine. Once earned, you do what you have to do to never disgrace that title. You commit your life to your fellow Marines. Semper fidelis, Latin for "always faithful," is not just a motto; it is a way of life for Marines. The Marine Corps is more than a bunch of longtime friends; it is a family that shares a bloodline bond that can't be broken.

My father was a flight engineer and top turret gunner flying in B-24s during World War II. I don't have any of his stories, not even any medals or trinkets. I do have a bunch of his pictures and the version of a DD214 used then. I regret never sitting with him and hearing his stories. I know there were many for a simple country boy from Cairo, Missouri. I don't want my stories to fade away with no one able to recount what I went through. This story is for my family and my squadron mates to share with their families.

When I started this simple story, I only had what I could remember. I was in intermittent contact with a couple of my former squadron mates via Facebook and was surprised when one of them passed away. In that passing, I saw a comment from another squadron mate, Tom Broderick, with whom I had lost contact. We both attended Auburn University on the degree completion program offered by the Marine Corps, and my wife and I had stayed with Tom and his family in Auburn when I was looking for a house. Tom was able to share after-action reports from Eagle Claw missions from January 1969 to June 1970 and a few addresses for other squadron mates from the Pop-A-Smoke organization. (It is amazing how little information we put in those after-action reports.) He also included some valuable information from the Pop-A-Smoke NOTAM Board.

I sent letters (real U.S. Mail–type letters) with my phone number and email address to everyone he had an address for. Then I started

57. Semper Fidelis

waiting. A week or two later, I got a couple of my letters back as undeliverable. I began thinking that the letter writing was a bust when I got my first email from a lost friend. That conversation led to a contribution to this story and contact information for another missing friend. Then over the next week or so, I got more emails leading to more contributions. Everyone I've talked to has been happy to offer contributions, some unique like "Night Fright or Which

HML-167 squadron patch.

HML-167 memorial, Quantico, Virginia.

Way Is Up?" and "Recon and Tigers—Oh My!" but mostly augmenting stories I was already familiar with. In any case, thanks for supplementing my vague recollections.

During a recent reunion of the squadron, it was suggested I check out the archives of Texas Tech University. That led to the command chronologies and after-action reports of every unit that served in Vietnam (and really supplemented my meager memory).

If this book interested you, here are some places and things you should check out. All Marines should visit the Museum of the Marine Corps, located at Quantico, Virginia, and if you are a member or former member of HML-167, visit the HML-167 Memorial at the Museum of the Marine Corps. Marine veterans of Vietnam should visit the Pop-A-Smoke website: **pop-a-smoke.com**.

Members and former members of that proud warrior squadron HML-167 should join the HML-167 Association at **hml167-hmla167.com**, free for former members of 167. Like "once a Marine, always a Marine," if you are 167, then "once a warrior, always a warrior."

Appendix A
Numbered Call Signs, After April 9, 1970

LtCol McCaughey	6		Lt Geaslin	33
Maj Thiesse	5		Lt Cole	34
Maj Merrill	1		Lt Hall	35
Maj Hooper	2		Lt Hunt	36
Maj Sharr	3		Lt Conner	37
Capt Adams	4		Lt Holland	38
Maj Martin	7		Lt Crew	39
Capt Eyre	8		Lt Thrasher	40
Capt Hammer	9		Lt Casner	41
Capt Blair	10		Lt Hugenberg	42
Lt Hutton	11		Lt Lockwood	43
Lt Hannon	12		Lt Graham	44
Lt Heiberg	14		Lt Clark	45
Lt Smith, M.A.	15		Lt Sykes	46
Lt Harris	16		Lt Davis	47
Lt Grandy	17		Lt Leaming	48
Lt Stevermer	18		Lt Dukelow	50
Lt Nelson	19		Lt Boulton	51
Lt Steele	20		Lt Bennett	52
Lt Jenkins	21		Lt North	53
Lt Gale	22		Lt Olshefski	54
Lt Myers	23		Lt Randall	55
Lt Fleener	24		Lt Scott, W.F.	56
Lt Smith, J.R.	25		Lt Watson	57
Lt Dodd	26		Lt Hinton	60
Lt Josten	27		Lt Boyer	71
Lt Hamilton	28		Lt Duemling	75
Capt Barr	29		Lt Miller	77
Lt Ohman	30		Lt Duesing	80
Lt Villano	31		Lt Worley	99
Lt Matthews	32			

Appendix B
III MAF Command Chronology Civic Action, August 1970

DECLASSIFIED

Aug 70

8. Civil Affairs

   a. *Objectives*. The basic objectives of the III Marine Amphibious Force Civic Affairs Program remain the same.

   b. *Civic Action Statistics*

   (1) Cost of supplies contributed from military resources for civic action projects (does not include cost of commodities obtained from USAID, CORDS, CRS, and like organizations): $VN 2,721,554

   (2) Expenditures from US/FWMAF Civic Action/PSYWAR Fund: $VN 231,955

   (3) Major Civic Action Programs:

	Man-days (10-hr days)	$VN
a. Economic Development	539	671,677
b. Education	203	486,700
c. Social Welfare	818	1,245,722
d. Transportation	369	295,240
e. Refugee Assistance Support	643	420,378

   (4) Number of separate institutions supported during the reporting period:

a. Schools	41
b. Orphanages	22
c. Hospitals/Dispensaries	20
d. Others	8

   (5) MEDCAP-DENTAL

   (a) Treatments

	Number of Patients
Medical	
Resulting from Hostile Action	194
Not resulting from Hostile Action	37,942

Enclosure (1)

DECLASSIFIED

DECLASSIFIED

Immunizations	469
Dental	868
Total	39,473

(b) Number of Vietnamese Health Workers Trained: 67

c. <u>Civic Action Projects</u>. The following are highlights of significant civic action projects conducted during the month of August 1970:

(1) 1st Marine Division reports the following:

(a) On 30Aug70, NVA troops attacked the An Hoa Buddhist Orphanange in Duc Duc District. The 5th Marines provided prompt medical treatment to the injured victims of the attack. The combined material and technical assistance from G-5 and the 5th Marines has hastened the prompt rebuilding of the orphanage.

(b) Though the greater part of time, work, and assistance has already been devoted to the completion of the Go Noi Island project from the 1st Marine Division, considerable progress has been made since the last reporting period. 1st Marine Division Reports:

1. 188 acres of land has been cleared.

2. 1.8 miles of road between village #1 and village #2 has been upgraded.

3. A "Pioneer Road" has been built 600 meters from village #2 to a small lake, which will serve as watering point for irrigation.

4. Gravel has been provided to upgrade three hundred meters of road from the bridge to village #1.

5. As of 15Aug70, 1,388 people were residing full time at village #1, while 150 inhabitants now occupy village 2.

(2) Force Logistic Command reports:

(a) The construction of wells, a community bath, and a continuing program of housing projects in the Hamlet of Phuoc Ha appear to be particularly effective because the people are offered the opportunity to aid one another and help the community as a whole. All projects are approved and coordinated through the appropriate hamlet officials. Maximum

DECLASSIFIED

Appendix B 215

DECLASSIFIED

participation is achieved by offering materials for personal use only to those individuals, who are willing to cooperate with the local program officials. This system helps strengthen the peoples' reliance upon their elected officials.

   (b) The construction of a market place in the hamlet of Hoa My exemplifies the improvements made toward initiating self-help projects. Funds were obtained through the 1970 Village Self-Development Program to build the market place. Such projects involve the participants in the decision making process within their local government, as well as the improvement of their community.

  (3) Combined Action Force reports:

   (a) CAP Marines of Dien Ban District have devoted recent efforts toward school construction and repair. Such programs have generated greater cooperation and understanding among local civilians, CAP Marines, and Popular Forces.

   (b) Combined Action Forces have also provided material assistance to refugee camps. Providing permanent wood siding for their houses, instead of cardboard or inferior materials, is helping villagers/refugees gain confidence in PF's.

Enclosure (1)

DECLASSIFIED

Appendix C
III MAF Command Chronology Civic Action, September 1970

Appendix C

DECLASSIFIED

SECRET
Sep 70

8. CIVIL AFFAIRS

   a. <u>Objectives</u>. The basic objectives of the III Marine Amphibious Force Civic Affairs Program remain the same.

   b. <u>Civic Action Statistics</u>

(1) Cost of supplies contributed from military resources for civic action projects (does not include cost of commodities obtained from USAID, CORDS, CRS, and like organizations): $VN 2,453,547

(2) Expenditures from US/FWMAF Civic Action/PSYWAR Fund:
$VN 204,410

(3) Major Civic Action Programs:

		Man-days (10-hr days)	$VN
a.	Economic Development	234	293,079
b.	Education	237	694,845
c.	Social Welfare	671	967,553
d.	Transportation	176	559,815
e.	Refugee Assistance Support	617	1,169,322

(4) Number of separate institutions supported during the reporting period:

a.	Schools	28
b.	Orphanages	13
c.	Hospitals/Dispensaries	14
d.	Others	8

(5) MEDCAP-DENTAL

   (a) <u>Treatments</u>

	Number of Patients
Medical	
Resulting from Hostile Action	109
Not resulting from Hostile Action	32,957

SECRET
Enclosure (1)

DECLASSIFIED

Appendix C

DECLASSIFIED

SECRET

```
        Immunizations                981
        Dental                       487
                          Total   34,534
```

(b) Number of Vietnamese Health Workers Trained: 64

c. <u>Civic Action Projects</u>. The following are highlights of significant civic action projects conducted during the month of September 1970:

(1) 1st Marine Aircraft Wing reports the following:

(a) To date, the 1st MAW Civic Action and Animal Husbandry Demonstration Center located in Phuoc Tuong Hamlet of Hoa Phat Village has 225 White Leghorn hens and 40 White Leghorn roosters. These were purchased on Okinawa as eggs or chicks, then incubated and grown in the Civic Action compound, and are presently being cared for by the Marine Civic Action Team and several Vietnamese. All feed is purchased at the Danang feed mill at a cost of 35 piasters per kilo. All medicine and vitamins are purchased in Danang and all specialized health care is provided by American civilian and military veterinarians.

The 225 hens are from 18 to 21 weeks old, depending upon when they were purchased. Purchase price for the eggs was 15 cents (U.S. currency) per egg and approximately 60 cents for each new born rooster. The eggs were placed in a 260 egg capacity incubator in the Phuoc Tuong Civic Action Center for a three week period. Hatch rate of the eggs purchased on Okinawa was between 75% to 85% and as high as 92%. The hatch rate for eggs purchased in Saigon by CORDS was generally around 35%. Approximately 90% of the hatched chicks were sold at one-half the local price to Vietnamese villagers interested in poultry production. These sales helped to defray the high cost of feed. All those who purchased chicks were informed of the veterinary services available to them at Hoa Vang District and Danang, and were encouraged to begin poultry raising rather than to immediately sell the chicks for a short-term profit.

At present approximately 60 hens are laying between 30 to 40 eggs daily. When enough eggs of sufficient size are laid, they will be incubated to determine their hatch rate. At that time, either eggs or chicks will be sold to any Civic Action unit or CORDS affiliated volunteer agency interested in poultry production. By the end of October of this year over 100 eggs daily is the expected rate of production. It is hoped that with a distribution of eggs such as this that at least a minor increase in poultry and poultry products will occur in Hoa Vang District.

SECRET

DECLASSIFIED

Appendix C

DECLASSIFIED

SECRET

A fire on the 24th of September in Hoa An Hamlet of Hoa Phat Village destroyed 18 houses leaving 145 Vietnamese homeless. 1st MAW provided emergency relief to the victims. A water trailer was left at the scene for three days; 80 cases of C-rations were given to and distributed by the hamlet chief; and 11th Motor Transport Battalion signed over four (4) General Purpose tents to be used as temporary shelter. Marines from both 1stMAW Civic Action and 11th Motor Transport Battalion Supply, together with the Popular Force militia of Hoa An Hamlet, erected two of the tents. One additional tent was provided and erected by the Vietnamese motor transport unit located near the scene of the fire.

Scrap lumber and tin are presently being collected to provide partial aid for the rebuilding of destroyed homes and property. The Hoa Vang District Civic Action Officer is also attempting to get construction commodities through GVN channels.

(2) 1st Marine Division reports:

(a) Due to the interest shown by Civic Action personnel of the 1st Marine Division, the villagers of Phuoc Thuan Hamlet, Hoa Vang District led the S-5 of Headquarters Battalion to a VC base camp and uncovered a VC rice cache.

The close cooperation by the villagers in conjunction with US and GVN efforts to construct 140 new homes and repair 80 other homes at Tu Cau and Ngan Cau Hamlets has convinced many people that the GVN is concerned about their welfare.

(3) Force Logistic Command reports:

(a) On 22 September 1970 at 0210 there was a fire in the hamlet of Hoa My. Three fire trucks from FLC and two fire trucks from 1st MAW responded to the call. One woman and two children (6year old girl and 8 year old boy) were fatally burned. There were no other casualties. The firemen worked for an hour and a half before the fire was completely out. Over 14,000 gallons of water were expended from the FLC fire trucks. The cause of the fire is still unknown.

Civil Affairs personnel of Maintenance Battalion, FLC delivered more than 30 truckloads of lumber, including plywood and 2x4's to the Hamlet Chief of Hoa My. This lumber will be used to rebuild the ten stores/dwellings destroyed by the fire.

SECRET

Enclosure (1)

DECLASSIFIED

Appendix D
Monthly Flight Time

October 1969	11.7	First Flight, October 27
November 1969	64.9	JEST School, 4 days
December 1969	69.9	
January 1970	70.8	R&R—Sydney, Australia
February 1970	72.3	
March 1970	74.1	Leave—Taipei, Taiwan
April 1970	63.2	
May 1970	93.5	Crew Rest—Udorn, Thailand
June 1970	88.6	
July 1970	87.1	
August 1970	86.9	
September 1970	66.4	Last Flight, September 28
Total	**849.4**	

Bibliography

Email and Phone Contributions from:

- Col Mike Smith
- LtCol Elmer Davis
- LtCol Larry Grandy
- LtCol Rick Jenkins
- LtCol Paul Pratt
- Maj Tom Broderick
- Capt Lynn Boyer
- Capt John Gale
- Capt Joel Hall
- Capt Milt Matthews

HML-167 After Action Reports, 15 Oct 1969–30 Sep 1970, The Vietnam Center and Sam Johnson Vietnam Archive: USMC Unit Documents, https://www.vietnam.ttu.edu/references/usmc/unit.php?unit=HML%20-%20167.

HML-167 Command Chronologies, Oct 1969–Sep 1970, The Vietnam Center and Sam Johnson Vietnam Archive: USMC Unit Documents, https://www.vietnam.ttu.edu/references/usmc/unit.php?unit=HML%20-%20167.

III MAF Command Chronologies, Aug–Sep 1970, The Vietnam Center and Sam Johnson Vietnam Archive: USMC Unit Documents, https://www.vietnam.ttu.edu/references/usmc/unit.php?unit=III%20MAF.

USMC/Vietnam Helicopter Association—KIA Database—NOTAM Board.

Walker, Harold G., *The Grotto*, Book One, Dragonfly Publishing.

Walker, Harold G., *The Grotto*, Book Two, Dragonfly Publishing.

Willis, Bud, *Marble Mountain: A Vietnam Memoir*, Authorhouse Publishing.

Index

American Red Cross 11, 87
An Hoa 100, 115–6, 128–9, 135–6, 139–40, 156–8, 163–4, 169–70, 188
Arizona 67, 72, 129, 139, 155

Bennett, John 174, 211
Boyer, Lynn 172–3, 211
Broderick, Tom 68, 77, 114, 117, 208, 221
Bugman, David 122

Casner, Lewis 174, 211
Castle, Robert 91, 111, 115–6

Davis, Elmer 68, 83, 90–1, 211, 221
DeLong, Mike 71
DMZ 124
Dodd, Richard 173–4, 211
Duemling, Ralph 187, 211

Fitzsimmons, "Cotton" 11

Gale, John 106, 109, 211, 221
Geaslin, David 173, 211
Goi Noi 101
Gonzales, David 116, 176
Graham, William 176, 211
Grandy, Larry 115–6, 211, 221

Hai Van Pass 117, 194–5
Hall, Joel 68, 74, 133, 211, 221
Hill 55 67, 72, 95, 100, 129
HML-167 56–8, 62–3, 70, 86, 89–90, 103, 111, 115, 166, 202, 209, 210, 221
HML-367 2, 58, 68, 84, 110, 112, 142, 166
HMM-161 86
HMM-262 86, 94
HMM-361 57
HMM-364 94, 100, 125
Hoi An 72

III MAF 2, 62, 64, 71, 97, 127, 135, 172, 179, 181, 190–1, 199, 200, 202, 212, 216, 221

Jenkins, Richard 60, 64, 68, 118, 211, 221
Johnson, Patricia 185, 187

Land of the Blue Dragon 67, 99, 102
LZ Baldy 67, 72, 98–9, 102, 118, 139, 155

MABS-31 22–3
MAG-16 56, 91, 130, 202–3
MAG-31 22–3
Marvelous Marve 68, 121, 139–41, 170
MATCU-69 22–6, 35, 203
Matthews, Milt 68, 80–1, 91, 163–5, 172, 211, 221
McCorkle, Fred 71
McCutcheon, Keith LtGen 127, 135, 179–80, 199, 202
Miller, Thomas BGen 75, 135, 179, 189, 194, 199–200, 202
Miss America 2, 185–7
Miss North Carolina 185, 187, 205
Miss Texas 185
Mission Commander 2, 74–5, 110–1, 115, 188
Moberly Area Community College 7–10
Museum of the Marine 210

Nelson, Ellis 160, 211
Nickerson, Hermon LtGen 127

Parsons, Larry 114–5, 118
Peppenheim, Thomas 198
Phu Bai 58, 72, 84, 86, 88, 110–2, 114, 117, 123, 185, 194
Plasterer, Ross 71
Pop-a-Smoke 98, 208, 210
Pratt, Paul 114–5, 211

Index

Que Son Mountains 72, 131, 157, 167

Rodgers, Johnny 174
RT 119, 145–6, 156–8, 170

Scagloine, PC 94
Shelton, Joe 198
Smith, David L 198
Smith, JR 68, 211
Smith, MA 68, 111, 211, 221

Underwood, Thomas 116
USO 2, 81–2, 88, 185–6, 202

VMO-2 57, 86
VMO-6 86

Walker, Harold 66, 72, 74, 94, 125, 127, 130–1, 221
Whiteside, Jim 72
Whiteside, Tom 72
Widdecke, CF MGen 127
Williams, Mike Gen 71

www.ingramcontent.com/pod-product-compliance
Ingram Content Group UK Ltd.
Pitfield, Milton Keynes, MK11 3LW, UK
UKHW041948140426
5217IPUK00014B/703